❦ Convertible Cooking for a Healthy Heart

Convertible Cooking for a Healthy Heart

HOW TO TURN YOUR FAVORITE RECIPES INTO LOW-FAT LOW-CHOLESTEROL DELICIOUS DISHES

Joanne D'Agostino, R.N., B.S.N., M.Ed.

IN COLLABORATION WITH

Frank J. D'Agostino, M.D., F.A.C.G.

A Lou Reda Book

Published by Hastings House/Healthy Heart
Mamaroneck, N.Y.

DEDICATED WITH LOVE
TO
Daddy and Loretta

Library of Congress Catalog Card Number 91-73926
ISBN: 0-8038-9338-8

Printed in the United States of America

Contents

🍂 A Note from the Author

The nutrient values found at the end of each recipe were obtained from food value charts, literature provided by the United States Department of Agriculture, and manufacturers' product labels.

Keep in mind that this book is not intended as a prescribed dietary program for a specific illness or condition. Individuals who require such a regime should, of course, consult their physicians. Furthermore, I make no recommendations as to the specific amount of fat or cholesterol or the number of calories one should consume in a day. Nutritional needs vary from person to person and should be determined by one's physician or other qualified medical professional.

🍒 *Acknowledgments*

With a sense of indebtedness, I declare my deepest gratitude and appreciation:

To my dear Heavenly Father, who provides the wisdom, strength, guidance, and direction to get me through an average day.

To Frank and Erica, who lend their ears when I need to vent, their hands when I'm tired, their patience when I'm unreasonable, their encouragement when I'm weary, and their unconditional love—always.

To Daddy and Loretta, whose support is constant and whose pride is genuine.

To Marie, Leo, Carmen, Janelle, and Jeffrey, for epitomizing the true meaning of "family."

To my extended family, for caring and for showing it.

Finally, to Lou, for making it all happen.

My sincere thanks,
Joanne

 *Foreword*

by Mark Bricklin
Editor, *Prevention* Magazine

"Wow! I can't believe this is low-fat chicken . . . it tastes like veal."

That was a typical comment heard when I first worked with Joanne D'Agostino.

It came from me, in fact. But many others were making similar comments of surprise and delight when Joanne was featured at the very first class of *Prevention* Magazine's School of Cooking for Health.

Her approach is disarmingly simple. Many of us are used to seeing famous chefs do all sorts of maneuvers, and using lots of unusual herbs to achieve high taste with low-fat cookery. Joanne is the first to admit she's no chef. But that turns out to be a strength, not a weakness. Her ideas, techniques, and recipes are so easy to follow that anyone can succeed in producing meal after meal that hits the health target right in the middle and scores a bull's-eye with your taste buds.

My advice is to make this book part of your core library for healthful eating. You'll find it easy to understand, easy to use, and full of practical but up-to-date wisdom.

Medical Commentary

by Frank J. D'Agostino, M.D., F.A.C.G.

The evidence implicating cholesterol and saturated fats as important causal factors for coronary artery disease is compelling and continues to mount. The so-called "cholesterol controversy" is no longer a controversy. Overwhelming justification for the association between high cholesterol and coronary artery disease has been established worldwide—epidemiologically, clinically, and experimentally. In addition, emigration studies and dietary intervention studies firmly support the association. Unfortunately, it appears that many individuals remain unconvinced.

One out of two Americans continues to die of cardiovascular disorders. More than 4,000 Americans suffer a heart attack daily. That adds up to 123,000 per month and 1,400,000 per year. One half million of these will die, 65 percent before they reach a hospital. How can we permit these events to continue?

It is disturbing that as mindful as we are of the cholesterol–saturated fat problem, 98 percent of men and women between ages 21–34 and 80 percent of men and women between ages 35–44 do not know their cholesterol levels. These men and women could be practicing a healthy life style of preventive medicine by monitoring their fat and cholesterol intake! Furthermore, according to the National Health and Nutrition Exam Study, 64 million people have cholesterol levels high enough to warrant advice and/or treatment.

Since 1928, thirteen Nobel prizes have been awarded to individuals for their remarkable research involving the cholesterol molecule. We have not taken full advantage of that wealth of information. In fact, the latest studies show that while Americans are eating less tropical oil, whole milk, beef, lard, and butter, they are increasing their intake of cheese, ice cream, sour cream, salad and cooking oils, and high-fat snacks.

Approximately three-quarters of the world's population eats a healthier diet than do Americans. Why? Most people cannot afford our "western-style" fat-laden, simple carbohydrate-refined food diet! People who live in poorer countries must rely on a high complex-carbohydrate diet of grains, vegetables, legumes, fruits, and fish, or similar foods that they can grow or gather on their own. Ironically, this seemingly modest diet is more in sync with our genetic make-up. It developed over several million years of human evolution and dates from when we were primarily hunter-gatherers of foods. Man has never been equipped to tolerate high levels of fat and cholesterol in his diet, body, or bloodstream.

The fact that a billion Chinese in an underdeveloped country—a country that can not boast the most advanced and sophisticated medical care in the world—live as long as we do is mind-boggling. The Chinese do not die of heart disease. In fact, their average cholesterol level is 90–125 mg/dl. Is their low-fat, low-cholesterol, high-carbohydrate diet the key to their longevity? There may be a deep-rooted lesson to be learned from these comparisons.

Atherosclerosis is a disease that builds up daily and is the result of a slow, silent, progressive, unrelenting, life-long process. It can cause clogging of all the major arteries affecting the brain, eyes, kidneys, extremities, and so on. What's more, so called "fatty streaks," early signs of atherosclerosis, have been documented in the aorta of nearly all American children over 3 years of age and in the coronary arteries of half the children 10–14 years of age who were studied at autopsies (studies conducted by Drs. R. Holman in 1961 and H. C. Stary in 1987 and recited in an article by Richard E. Garcia, M.D., and Douglas S. Moodie, M.D., published in the Cleveland Clinic Journal of Medicine, Nov.–Dec. 1990). A child who has a high-cholesterol level matures into an adult with a high-cholesterol level. We must begin to show greater concern regarding their diet.

In April 1991 the government finally developed new guidelines for children. Starting at age 2 or 3, a toddler's eating habits should begin to approach those of older family members. Basic rules remain the same: Total fat intake should not exceed 30 percent of total daily calories with saturated fats (the real culprits) comprising only one-third, or 10 percent of that amount. Cholesterol intake should remain limited to less than 300 milligrams a day.

The recipes in this book do better than that. They consistently remain well below these government recommendations, thereby providing a safety feature for those who occasionally find a high-fat meal unavoidable, as when dining out or attending a party.

Remember that a diet low in cholesterol and saturated fat can reduce heart fatalities and cardiovascular events. Numerous recent reports from worldwide medical authorities and centers indicate that such diets can slow down the progress of coronary lesions and, more astonishingly, can actually cause regression or resolution (disappearance) of atherosclerotic lesions. What a remarkable breakthrough!

So, take charge of your health. Become informed. Learn about nutrition. Discuss it with your neighbor, your co-worker, your relative. Talk it up. Develop healthy eating habits and a healthier life style. Make it a family affair. Involve the children. Get motivated, and stay that way. It's the secret to a long and healthy life!

Introduction

My first book, *Italian Cooking for a Healthy Heart*, was written in response to a crisis. My husband Frank developed coronary artery disease in 1986, underwent angioplasty, and was advised by his cardiologist to follow a strict, low-fat, low-cholesterol diet. Finding an appropriate diet cookbook was not a problem. The bookstores were well stocked with a vast array of books boasting the secret to solving the cholesterol problem through the preparation of cholesterol-lowering, heart-healthy foods. However, finding one that would work for us was another problem!

In retrospect, the situation that contributed to Frank's cardiac incident had been brewing for many years. His cholesterol level averaged 250–290 milligrams for twenty years or longer. At the time, he was completing his fellowship in gastroenterology at the University of Pennsylvania, an environment in which access to the most current medical research was readily available. During those years a 250–290 milligram cholesterol level was considered to be well within the normal range. One of Frank's professors, who was doing in-depth research on the issue of the cholesterol–heart disease–nutrition link, suggested that he begin a nutritional program designed to reduce his cholesterol level to at most 200 milligrams. So, while the rest of the world, including most of the medical profession, believed that a cholesterol level of 280 or 290 milligrams was acceptable, Frank and I began our first attempt at reducing his level through diet modification. Unfortunately, we soon learned that adherence to such diets was short-lived for several reasons. First, our best efforts at limiting cholesterol intake produced only minimal improvement in Frank's blood cholesterol level. Second, the foods were dull and lacked taste appeal. Thus, our failure to obtain results soon led to frustration, followed by discouragement, and ultimately a return to old eating habits. Nevertheless, we repeated the above scenario over and over again during the years preceding Frank's cardiac incident, because we needed to feel that we were at least trying to effect a positive change. We were, however, unsuccessful.

In fact, it was not until after the trauma of Frank's illness in 1986 that the urgency of the situation became evident. Previously, dietary change was something we toyed with voluntarily. Suddenly, it was imperative that we change. Faced with a crisis situation, we armed ourselves with the latest research on the relationship between diet and cholesterol, and embarked on a mission to declare war on the excess fat and cholesterol in our diet. What began as a personal vendetta, culminated in a technique of food preparation that not only brought positive results, but also led to my first book.

Without a doubt, the first recipes developed were not only instrumental in lowering Frank's cholesterol by 100 milligrams in a three-week period, but, more important, they served as a reminder that low-fat, low-cholesterol cooking does not have to be synonymous with terrible taste. That was the key to our successful attempt to lower Frank's cholesterol level and keep it down. The taste of the food was very important. After having bounced from diet to diet over the years, we were living proof of that assessment.

Moreover, we learned that there was much more to coronary artery disease than high cholesterol. An individual's cholesterol level might be well within the acceptable norm (which by 1987 had been revised downward to 200 milligrams), but because of a genetic predisposition or other risk factors, such as hypertension, diabetes, obesity, smoking, and so on, he or she may still fall victim to heart disease.

Whatever the reason for coronary artery disease, one thing became more and more evident—dietary changes were an integral part of both the prevention and treatment. More specifically, we learned that it was not enough simply to read labels for cholesterol content of foods. Of equal importance was the need to reduce the amount of total fat in the diet—not just saturated fat—but TOTAL fat.

In retrospect, it was probably naïveté to think that Frank and I could succeed in our "fat surgery" mission, when the research showed that about 50 percent of the calories consumed in a day by the average American are fat calories. Despite the dubious odds, the months of research, label reading, and recipe testing paid off. Not only did Frank's cholesterol level drop, it remained down! The secret? He found it easy to stay on his diet. Why? He was still eating his favorite Italian cuisine. The delicious flavors that kept him coming back for more were still there. The only missing ingredient was the fat!

That was the background of the first book. Judging by its immediate success, others found it beneficial for their needs, as well. Following the simple logic, that if people could continue to eat low-fat, low-cholesterol versions of foods they found appealing, they would be less inclined to hop from one unsuccessful diet to another. So, my next self-imposed assignment was to convince people that they did not have to forsake all their favorite meals. Instead, all they had to do was to learn the art of "conversion," or recipe modification—a new twist to old recipes.

As a columnist for the *Express*, my hometown newspaper, I was given the opportunity to demonstrate my technique of recipe conversion by taking traditional recipes and revamping them into acceptable low-fat, low-cholesterol versions. A few of the recipe revisions that appeared in my weekly column were based on favorites from my first book. Therefore, variations of a few also appear in this book. However, it wasn't long before I began experimenting with a few that offered greater challenges. Several columns were based on readers' requests for revisions of their favorite meals. In fact, there was such a terrific response locally that many readers began making copies of the columns and sending them to their out-of-town family members and friends, many of whom had *Italian Cooking for a Healthy Heart* and wanted to use the columns as an addendum to the book. Thus, the impetus for *Convertible Cooking for a Healthy Heart* evolved.

This book represents a compilation of my columns for the past year. In many respects, it provides different information from my first book because, in every case, both the traditional version of the recipe and the low-fat revision are provided. Additionally, a short explanation precedes each recipe renovation, reviewing the substitutions and the net results and nutritional benefits of the conversion. As in the first book, the nutrient values per serving are given at the end of each recipe to aid those who wish to keep tabs on calories, fat, and cholesterol intake per meal.

Certain themes and ingredient substitutions repeat themselves throughout the book. They include: the elimination of all added fats, such as butter, oil, and margarine in the cooking process; the use of low-fat dairy products; the substitution of poultry and fish for recipes traditionally calling for red meat; the use of Butter Buds, a nonfat butter substitute; and the use of non-cholesterol egg substitute. The consistent use of these substitute ingredients render the recipes that follow among the lowest in fat, cholesterol, and calories than any similar collection currently in print. Although most experts recommend restricting total dietary fat intake per day to 30 percent of total calories, most of the following recipes are well under 20 percent, and in many cases under 10 percent! Note that salt has not been completely eliminated from the recipes in the book. Individuals who, on the advice of their physicians, have been advised to restrict sodium intake, may wish to omit salt from the recipes. In most cases, the use of salt is optional. After reviewing the methods employed in each case of converting the traditional recipe to a heart-healthy version, you should feel well equipped to take your favorite recipe and, through appropriate substitutions, create an acceptable, nutritionally sound adaptation of that recipe.

Clearly, cooking for a healthy heart does not mean sitting in the kitchen with a calculator tallying up grams of fat and milligrams of cholesterol. It is, instead, a commitment to a life style change with regard to food selection and preparation methods. I repeat—it does not mean you must abandon your favorite foods, but you must find healthier ways to prepare them.

I have carefully and purposely avoided the technical side of this timely issue of dietary fat and cholesterol. Aside from a brief medical commentary and update by my husband Frank, I've tried to keep this book as simple and straightforward as possible. Much like *Italian Cooking for a Healthy Heart*, this book is designed for the person who does the cooking. Frankly, enough has been said by other authors and the media about the medical advantages of a prudent low-fat, low-cholesterol diet. Modern medicine positively states that a low-fat diet can help prevent heart disease, decrease our risk of certain types of cancer, promote weight loss, and help in the treatment of certain other diseases, such as high blood pressure and diabetes. There are volumes of material available in the library for the reader who is interested in the scientific and biochemical aspects of this topic.

This book should serve, first, as a kitchen aid to help you achieve your goal of cutting back on some of the unnecessary fat and cholesterol in your diet. Second, use it as a guide for easy-to-prepare, heart-healthy meals that will get you in and out of the kitchen quickly. Finally, it should serve as an educational tool by challenging you to apply the techniques that I have used in my conversions to prepare your own healthy recipes. Have fun, good luck, and *buon appetito!*

SOUPS
AND
PASTAS

 **Seafood Bisque**

If you love French cuisine, you are undoubtedly familiar with the golden touch of French chefs when it comes to the preparation of rich, creamy wine sauces and soups. They demonstrate a certain savvy matched by no one in their creation of shellfish soups. Such is the case with Seafood Bisque, a thick French soup usually made from shellfish and a substantial amount of butter and cream—the latter two of which are undeniably lethal ingredients on a low-fat, low-cholesterol diet!

Hooked on Seafood Bisque from the gourmet taste of my past, and not about to abandon that taste, I accepted the challenge of converting the recipe to a suitable heart-healthy alternative. The result is the low-fat recipe that follows.

The use of shellfish, such as lobster, crabmeat, or shrimp poses no problem when portions are kept reasonably moderate. Although some shellfish have a reputation for containing a greater amount of cholesterol than other types of fish, most still contain less per average serving than red meat. Moreover, they are much lower in saturated fat than red meat.

The use of butter and cream in the original Seafood Bisque recipe is another story, however. In the conversion, Butter Buds is used in place of butter, and evaporated skim milk replaces the light cream. Both serve as suitable substitutes for their high-fat counterparts, and provide enough "richness" to the recipe to satisfy even my taste.

Now for those who need an additional nudge to try the low-fat version of this recipe, check the food value numbers at the end of each recipe—especially fat content—and let your conscience direct you!

Traditional Recipe

8 tablespoons butter
½ pound seafood (lobster, crabmeat, shrimp)
½ cup chopped onions
½ cup chopped celery
½ cup flour
¼ cup cooking sherry
1 teaspoon paprika
2 tablespoons tomato purée
salt and pepper to taste (optional)
1 quart chicken broth or fish stock
1 cup light cream

Low-Fat Version

Butter Buds equivalent to 8 tablespoons butter
¼ cup cooking sherry
½ pound seafood (lobster, crabmeat, shrimp)
½ cup chopped onions
½ cup chopped celery
½ cup flour
1 teaspoon paprika
2 tablespoons tomato purée
salt and pepper to taste (optional)
1 quart defatted chicken broth or fish stock
1 cup evaporated skim milk

In a medium soup pot or kettle, sauté seafood, onions, and celery in butter until tender. Sprinkle with flour and stir in sherry, blending well. Next, stir in paprika, tomato purée, salt, pepper, and about ½ cup broth. Place mixture in food processor and purée until smooth. Return mixture to soup kettle. Add remaining broth and light cream. Heat, stirring constantly, until piping hot. Serve immediately. (Serves 6)

PER SERVING

Calories:	357
Fat:	29 grams
Cholesterol:	121 milligrams

Dissolve dry Butter Buds in sherry and place in medium soup pot or kettle with seafood, onions, and celery. Cook over medium heat until tender. Remove from heat and stir in flour until well-blended. Add paprika, tomato purée, salt, pepper, and about ½ cup broth. Mix well. Place mixture in food processor and purée until smooth. Return mixture to soup kettle. Add remaining broth and evaporated skim milk. Heat, stirring constantly, until piping hot. Serve immediately. (Serves 6)

PER SERVING

Calories:	138
Fat:	0.5 gram
Cholesterol:	30 milligrams

🍒 *Sweet Potato Bisque*

If you like sweet potatoes and cream soups, you'll probably enjoy Sweet Potato Bisque. This unusual soup can legitimately boast a richness, not only in taste, but also in vitamin and mineral content. Nutritionally speaking, a sweet potato is a real bonanza. It contains vitamin A in the form of beta-carotene, a nutrient known for its cancer prevention potential. The recommended dietary allowance for vitamin A is 5000 international units daily. However, many authorities believe that to maximize the anti-cancer protection in vitamin A we should consume about 12,500 international units per day. A cup of mashed sweet potatoes provides about 43,000 international units.

If you try the Sweet Potato Bisque, I suggest you choose the heart-healthy version, which provides the richness of the traditional version without the fat and calories. The use of light cream and butter in the traditional recipe triples the calories per serving and causes the fat content to soar from less than 1 gram to 23 grams per serving! Consequently, for the heart-healthy version I replaced these ingredients with low-fat substitutes. The finished product is even more nutritious than the original, and it tastes wonderful!

Traditional Recipe

8 tablespoons butter
½ cup chopped onions
1 cup chopped celery
2 large sweet potatoes, peeled and diced
3 cups chicken stock
⅛ teaspoon black pepper
salt to taste
½ cup light cream

Low-Fat Version

Butter Buds equivalent to 8 tablespoons butter
¼ cup water
½ cup chopped onions
1 cup chopped celery
2 large sweet potatoes, peeled and diced
3 cups defatted chicken broth
⅛ teaspoon black pepper
salt to taste (optional)
½ cup evaporated skim milk

Melt butter in Dutch oven or soup kettle. Add onions and celery, and sauté until tender. Add diced sweet potatoes and chicken stock. Cover and cook until potatoes are well done. Remove from heat and cool slightly. Pour potato mixture into food processor or blender and purée. (This may have to be done in several batches due to quantity.) Pour mixture back into Dutch oven. Add pepper and salt, if desired. Stir in light cream. Reheat and serve. (Serves 6)

PER SERVING

Calories:	275
Fat:	23 grams
Cholesterol:	70 milligrams

Combine Butter Buds and water and blend until smooth. Place into a nonstick Dutch oven or soup kettle with onions and celery. Sauté until tender. Add diced sweet potatoes and chicken broth. Cover and cook until potatoes are well done. Remove from heat and cool slightly. Pour mixture into food processor or blender and purée. (This may have to be done in several batches due to quantity.) Pour mixture back into Dutch oven. Add pepper and salt, if desired. Stir in evaporated skim milk. Reheat and serve. (Serves 6)

PER SERVING

Calories:	90
Fat:	0.3 gram
Cholesterol:	less than 1 milligram

Pasta with Broccoli and Shrimp

Pasta with Broccoli and Shrimp is an unusual one-dish meal that offers ease of preparation along with nutritional soundness for adventuresome individuals who are willing to try a slightly offbeat pasta dish. This dish may be especially appealing to you if you enjoy spaghetti and other Italian foods but find that tomato sauce doesn't always agree with you. Let me warn you though; this is not your typical spaghetti dish. That is, your pasta will not be swimming in a loose sauce. In fact, the finished product is more like a hot pasta salad rather than a typical spaghetti with sauce.

Two versions of the recipe follow. I used the traditional recipe for many years before I set out on a mission to eliminate the unnecessary fat in cooking. You will notice that both versions of this recipe are identical, except for two ingredients. Olive oil and butter are used in the original recipe. However, in the revised, low-fat recipe, white wine replaces the oil for sautéing, and Butter Buds is used instead of butter. The significance of these substitutions is evident when you compare the nutrient values of each recipe. Moreover, the change in taste is imperceptible, which leaves me with the conclusion that the butter and oil in the traditional recipe add nothing to this dish but calories, fat, and cholesterol!

Traditional Recipe

1 medium stalk broccoli, chopped
1 cup water
salt to taste, if desired
2 tablespoons olive oil
½ cup minced onions
2 tablespoons butter
2 cloves garlic, minced
10 large cooked shrimp (each cut into 3 pieces)
¼ cup white wine
¼ teaspoon oregano
½ teaspoon dried sweet basil
8 ripe olives, pitted and minced
crushed red pepper to taste, if desired
1 pound spaghetti, cooked

Low-Fat Version

1 medium stalk broccoli, chopped
½ cup chopped onions
salt to taste, if desired
1 cup water
¼ cup white wine
Butter Buds equivalent to 2 tablespoons butter
2 cloves garlic, minced
10 large cooked shrimp (each cut into 3 pieces)
¼ teaspoon oregano
½ teaspoon dried sweet basil
8 ripe olives, pitted and minced
crushed red pepper to taste, if desired
1 pound spaghetti, cooked

In a medium saucepan combine broccoli, water, and salt (if desired). Bring to a boil, reduce heat, cover, and simmer until broccoli is tender. In a large skillet, sauté onions in oil until tender. Add cooked broccoli and juice. Mix well and set aside. In a small skillet, melt butter. Add garlic and sauté until golden brown. Add shrimp and continue cooking for 2 or 3 minutes. Add wine, oregano, basil, minced olives, and crushed pepper (if desired). Blend well and add to large skillet containing broccoli. Mix well and cook over low heat for another 3 or 4 minutes. Arrange cooked pasta on a large platter. Spoon broccoli and shrimp mixture over pasta and serve while hot. (Serves 6)

PER SERVING

Calories:	319
Fat:	10.3 grams
Cholesterol:	29 milligrams

In a large, nonstick skillet, combine broccoli, onions, salt (if desired), and water. Cover and cook over medium heat until tender. Meanwhile, in a small, nonstick skillet, sauté garlic and shrimp in Butter Buds and 2 tablespoons of the wine for about 3 or 4 minutes. Next, add oregano, basil, minced olives, remaining wine, and crushed red pepper (if desired). Blend well and add to large skillet containing broccoli. Mix thoroughly and cook over medium heat for an additional 3 or 4 minutes. Arrange cooked pasta on large platter. Spoon broccoli and shrimp mixture over pasta and serve while hot. (Serves 6)

PER SERVING

Calories:	245
Fat:	1.8 grams
Cholesterol:	16 milligrams

🍅 Stir-Fry Medley with Pasta

My introduction to the original version of this Stir-Fry Medley with Pasta dish occurred about eight years ago. At the time, there was a rather significant emphasis on the merits of reducing cholesterol and saturated fat intake, but there was little concern for reducing the total dietary fat, which we now know is equally important. In keeping with the experts' advice, I made appropriate substitutions to the original recipe and prepared what seemed to be a nutritionally sound pasta meal. At that time, because I was still using lean cuts of veal and beef in small portions, this recipe fit our life style, with the exception of the use of butter. Thus, the only modification I made was to substitute a polyunsaturated margarine for the butter. While this change reduced the saturated fat and cholesterol in the recipe, it did nothing to reduce the total fat content.

Several years later I realized that to reduce effectively the total fat, as well as the cholesterol, a few additional changes were necessary. I replaced the veal with chicken breast; I used wine and pineapple juice to sauté; I eliminated oil; and I replaced both butter and margarine with Butter Buds. These changes netted some rather significant reductions in calories, fat, and cholesterol, as is evident by the nutrient values listed with the recipes below.

Traditional Recipe

½ pound thinly sliced veal cutlets
2 tablespoons vegetable oil
4 tablespoons butter
2 scallions, finely chopped
2 cups broccoli flowerettes
2 cups cauliflower flowerettes
½ teaspoon onion powder
salt and pepper to taste
2 tablespoons crushed pineapple
2 tablespoons pineapple juice
1 pound spaghetti, cooked

Low-Fat Version

½ pound thinly sliced boneless chicken breast cutlets
3 tablespoons white wine
½ cup pineapple juice
2 scallions, finely chopped
2 cups broccoli flowerettes
2 cups cauliflower flowerettes
Butter Buds equivalent to 2 tablespoons butter
½ teaspoon onion powder
dash or 2 of low sodium soy sauce
2 tablespoons crushed pineapple
1 pound spaghetti, cooked

Slice veal cutlets into strips about 3/8-inch by 1½ inches. Heat oil in a large skillet or wok. Add veal and stir-fry on high heat until brown. With a slotted spoon, remove veal from skillet and set aside. Add butter to skillet and heat until melted. Add scallions, broccoli, and cauliflower. Stir-fry on high heat until vegetables are cooked to the crisp-tender stage. Season with onion powder, salt, and pepper. Add crushed pineapple, pineapple juice, and veal. Toss over medium heat until all ingredients are well-blended and hot. Arrange cooked pasta on a large platter or pasta bowl. Spoon stir-fry medley over pasta and serve hot. (Serves 6)

PER SERVING

Calories:	429
Fat:	18.8 grams
Cholesterol:	62 milligrams

Slice chicken breast cutlets, crosswise, into 3/8-inch strips. In a large, nonstick skillet or wok, heat wine. Add chicken and cook on high, stirring constantly, until wine evaporates and chicken begins to adhere to skillet. Then add 2 or 3 tablespoons of pineapple juice to deglaze and loosen any residue adhering to the skillet. (Juices and chicken should have a rich brown color at this point.) With a slotted spoon, remove chicken from skillet and set aside. Pour remaining pineapple juice into skillet and heat to bubbling stage. Add scallions, broccoli, and cauliflower, and toss to coat with juice. Add Butter Buds, onion powder, and soy sauce. Stir-fry to crisp-tender stage. Add crushed pineapple and cooked chicken. Toss over medium heat until all ingredients are well-blended and hot. Arrange cooked pasta on large platter or pasta bowl. Spoon stir-fry medley over pasta and serve hot. (Serves 6)

PER SERVING

Calories:	317
Fat:	2.9 grams
Cholesterol:	29 milligrams

Linguini with Tuna

Since both my parents worked in the family restaurant business my sister Marie and I had to assume some of the household duties, particularly on weekends. Because I was older than Marie, I was able to use the stove and she was relegated to the after dinner clean-up. Friday was often my night to prepare the family dinner. When I was a teenager, Friday was fish night, and my Friday night contribution to the dinner table was frequently linguini with tuna fish sauce. Although tuna seems a perfect choice for a low-fat diet, when you begin the sauce with several cloves of garlic and a layer of olive oil you are well on your way to offsetting the benefits of the low-fat tuna. Also, if you use tuna packed in oil, you add about 65 grams of unnecessary fat to that pot of tuna fish sauce.

Revising this recipe was a cinch! All I did was to eliminate the oil used in the sauté process and substitute water-packed tuna for the oil-packed variety. Take it from one who has years of eating experience when it comes to tuna sauce, the lighter version is just as satisfying as the one that captured my taste buds many years ago. Here is a classic example of my contention that a heart-healthy diet does not mean trashing your favorite recipes. It's simply a matter of adapting them to conform to your new standards.

Traditional Recipe

- 2 tablespoons olive oil
- 2 cloves garlic, minced
- ½ cup minced onions
- 1 28-ounce can crushed tomatoes
- 1 6-ounce can tomato paste
- 1½ cups water
- 2 tablespoons chopped fresh parsley
- ½ teaspoon dried sweet basil
  crushed red pepper, if desired
- 2 6½-ounce cans tuna in oil
- 1 pound linguini, cooked

Low-Fat Version

- 2 tablespoons white wine
- 2 cloves garlic, minced
- ½ cup minced onions
- 1 28-ounce can crushed tomatoes
- 1 6-ounce can tomato paste
- 1½ cups water
- 2 tablespoons chopped fresh parsley
- ½ teaspoon dried sweet basil
  crushed red pepper, if desired
- 2 6½-ounce cans water-packed tuna (drained)
- 1 pound linguini, cooked

Heat oil in a medium saucepan. Add garlic and onions and simmer until tender. Add crushed tomatoes, tomato paste, water, parsley, basil, and pepper (if desired), blending thoroughly. Bring to a boil. Reduce heat, cover, and simmer for 10 minutes. Add tuna fish, cover, and simmer for about 20 minutes longer. Spoon sauce over cooked linguini and serve hot. (Serves 6)

PER SERVING

Calories:	428
Fat:	13.5 grams
Cholesterol:	36 milligrams

In a medium saucepan, sauté garlic and onions in wine until tender. Add crushed tomatoes, tomato paste, water, parsley, basil, and pepper (if desired), blending thoroughly. Bring to a boil. Reduce heat, cover, and simmer for 10 minutes. Add tuna fish, cover, and simmer for about 20 minutes longer. Spoon sauce over cooked linguini and serve hot. (Serves 6)

PER SERVING

Calories:	319
Fat:	2 grams
Cholesterol:	36 milligrams

Rigatoni with Sausage and Eggplant

Contrary to the opinion of many junk food addicts, embarking on a course of healthy eating is not synonymous with "giving up" all delicious food. Admittedly, there was a time when I questioned whether it was possible to make a delicious low-fat meal. When I first began experimenting with recipe conversions, I frequently found myself rechecking the recipe for fear that I had, inadvertently, added a forbidden "high-fat" ingredient. The food, it seemed, often tasted too good to be low in fat! At that time, the house rule was: "If it tastes too good, we probably shouldn't be eating it." My prior experience with low-fat diets had reinforced this sentiment. Fortunately, however, some things can be changed and even improved with a little effort.

The following revised recipe for Rigatoni with Sausage and Eggplant drives home the point that low-fat, low-cholesterol cuisine does not necessarily have to translate into low-flavor. The substitution of turkey sausage for pork sausage eliminates a substantial quantity of fat, without noticeably altering the taste. The use of rose wine in place of oil reduces the fat further and actually adds flavor that was lacking in the traditional version. The Parmesan cheese in the original recipe was overpowered by the other spicy flavors; so, when it is eliminated in the converted recipe, its absence is barely detectable.

All considered, the changes do little to alter the taste of this flavor-packed pasta dish. In fact, I still have difficulty convincing my family that it's a low-fat meal.

Traditional Recipe

½ pound pork sausage
¼ cup olive oil
2 cloves garlic, minced
1 onion, chopped
1 small eggplant, cubed (about ½ pound)
1 tablespoon chopped fresh parsley
1 tablespoon chopped fresh basil
⅛ teaspoon crushed red pepper (optional)
2 tablespoons grated Parmesan cheese
1 28-ounce can crushed tomatoes in purée
1 6-ounce can tomato paste
2 cups water
⅛ teaspoon baking soda
1 pound rigatoni, cooked

Low-Fat Version

½ pound lean turkey sausage
¼ cup rose wine
1 onion, chopped
1 small eggplant, cubed (about ½ pound)
2 cloves garlic, minced
1 tablespoon chopped fresh basil
⅛ teaspoon crushed red pepper (optional)
1 28-ounce can crushed tomatoes in purée
1 6-ounce can tomato paste
2 cups water
⅛ teaspoon baking soda
1 pound rigatoni, cooked

Place sausage in large skillet. Cover with water and parboil for about 15 minutes. Drain and cool. Cut into bite-size pieces and set aside.

Heat olive oil in a large saucepan. Add garlic and onion, and sauté until golden. Add eggplant, parsley, basil, and red pepper, if desired. Continue cooking over medium heat for about 2–3 minutes. Then, add sausage and cook for 10 minutes longer, stirring frequently. Sprinkle grated cheese over eggplant mixture and toss. Add crushed tomatoes, tomato paste, water, and baking soda. Blend thoroughly. Cover and simmer for 45 minutes, stirring occasionally. Serve over cooked rigatoni. (Serves 6)

PER SERVING

Calories: 515
Fat: 22.4 grams
Cholesterol: 36 milligrams

Place sausage in large skillet. Cover with water and parboil for about 15 minutes. Drain and cool. Cut into bite-size pieces and set aside.

In a large saucepan, combine wine, onion, eggplant, garlic, parsley, basil, and red pepper, if desired. Sauté over medium heat for about 2–3 minutes. Add sausage and cook for 10 minutes longer, stirring frequently. Add crushed tomatoes, tomato paste, water, and baking soda. Blend thoroughly. Cover and simmer for 45 minutes, stirring occasionally. Serve over cooked rigatoni. (Serves 6)

PER SERVING

Calories: 342
Fat: 4.8 grams
Cholesterol: 21 milligrams

Skipper's Linguini

The traditional version of Skipper's Linguini is an excellent example of a wolf in sheep's clothing, from a dietary standpoint. At quick glance, it appears to have the makings of a healthy seafood pasta meal. However, high-fat ingredients have turned this recipe into a dieter's nightmare. Bacon, butter, and cheese are the culprits, adding 18 grams of fat to each serving, along with a considerable increase in calories and cholesterol.

In the low-fat version of Skipper's Linguini, the bacon is replaced with turkey ham, while Butter Buds serves as the replacement for butter. The Parmesan cheese is simply eliminated. White wine, in place of bacon drippings, is used to sauté the onions and garlic. Also, although the traditional version of this recipe does not call for salt, the revised version recommends salt to taste. The original recipe ingredients provide ample amounts of salt, but once these ingredients are removed, a little extra salt may be needed to adjust for taste. When you consider the fat and salt you have eliminated by removing the bacon, butter, and cheese, a sprinkle of either regular or lite salt seems an acceptable trade-off—even for those who are attempting to limit salt intake.

Traditional Recipe

6 slices bacon, cut into ½-inch strips
¼ cup sliced scallions
2 cloves garlic, minced
6 tablespoons butter, melted
2 6½-ounce cans minced clams
1 6½-ounce can oil-packed tuna
½ cup sliced pitted ripe olives
¼ cup chopped parsley
⅛ teaspoon pepper
1 pound linguini, cooked
2 tablespoons grated Parmesan cheese

Low-Fat Version

1 ounce finely minced turkey ham
2 tablespoons white wine
¼ cup sliced scallions
2 cloves garlic, minced
Butter Buds equivalent to 6 tablespoons butter
2 6½-ounce cans minced clams
1 6½-ounce can water-packed light tuna
½ cup sliced pitted ripe olives
¼ cup chopped parsley
⅛ teaspoon pepper
salt to taste
1 pound linguini, cooked

In a skillet, cook bacon until crisp. Drain bacon, reserving ¼ cup drippings in skillet. Cook scallions and garlic in bacon drippings until tender, but not brown. Stir in melted butter. Add bacon, clams, tuna, olives, parsley, and pepper. Heat thoroughly. Pour over platter of hot, cooked linguini. Sprinkle with Parmesan cheese. (Serves 6)

PER SERVING

Calories:	467
Fat:	23.1 grams
Cholesterol:	93 milligrams

In a nonstick skillet, dry sauté minced turkey ham until brown, stirring constantly to prevent sticking. Remove ham from skillet and add wine. Sauté scallions and garlic in wine until tender. Dilute Butter Buds in about ¼ cup water, and add to skillet. Add turkey ham, clams, tuna, olives, parsley, pepper, and salt. Heat thoroughly. Pour over platter of hot, cooked linguini. (Serves 6)

PER SERVING

Calories:	295
Fat:	2.6 grams
Cholesterol:	50 milligrams

🍒 Spaghetti with Bolognese-Style Ragu

The city of Bologna, Italy, is known for its superb Italian cuisine. One of their specialities, Spaghetti with Bolognese-Style Ragu, has become a popular American favorite. A unique trademark of a Bolognese spaghetti sauce is the enrichment of the tomato sauce through the addition of butter and cream. Naturally, on a heart-healthy diet, these additions can be liabilities rather than assets, since both ingredients contain generous quantities of fat and cholesterol. However, with a few minor adaptations, individuals who are concerned about their fat and cholesterol intake can continue to enjoy this Italian favorite.

In the low-fat version, ground turkey replaces ground beef to reduce the saturated fat content. Also, the vegetables are sautéed by a method known as "dry sauté." The vegetables and ground turkey are cooked in their own juices, which allows for the elimination of the olive oil and butter, further reducing the total fat, calories, and cholesterol. Butter Buds is used to compensate for the flavor lost by the elimination of the olive oil and butter. Butter Buds replaces the rich, buttery "fat" taste without the calories and cholesterol. Evaporated skim milk serves as an excellent low-fat substitute for the light cream used in the original recipe. Clearly, the most obvious health benefit of the revised version of this recipe is the drastic reduction in total dietary fat.

Traditional Recipe

3 tablespoons olive oil
1 tablespoon butter
$\frac{1}{2}$ cup chopped onions
$\frac{1}{2}$ cup chopped carrots
$\frac{1}{4}$ cup chopped celery
1 pound ground beef
$\frac{1}{2}$ teaspoon salt (or to taste)
$\frac{1}{4}$ teaspoon pepper
1 28-ounce can crushed
   tomatoes
1 6-ounce can tomato paste
1 cup water
3 tablespoons light cream
1 pound spaghetti, cooked

Low-Fat Version

$\frac{1}{2}$ cup chopped onions
$\frac{1}{2}$ cup chopped carrots
$\frac{1}{4}$ cup chopped celery
1 pound ground turkey
$\frac{1}{2}$ teaspoon salt (or to taste)
$\frac{1}{4}$ teaspoon pepper
1 28-ounce can crushed
   tomatoes
1 6-ounce can tomato paste
1 cup water
3 tablespoons evaporated
   skim milk
   Butter Buds equivalent to 1
   tablespoon butter
1 pound spaghetti, cooked

In a large skillet, heat the olive oil and butter. Add the chopped onions, carrots, and celery. Sauté until tender. Add crumbled ground beef, salt, and pepper and cook until the meat is well done, stirring frequently. Combine crushed tomatoes, tomato paste, water, and cream and add to vegetables and beef. Blend thoroughly. Cover and simmer for 45 minutes, stirring occasionally. Serve over cooked spaghetti. (Serves 6)

PER SERVING

Calories:	524
Fat:	25.5 grams
Cholesterol:	65 milligrams

In a large, nonstick skillet, dry sauté onions, carrots, and celery until tender. Add crumbled ground turkey, salt, and pepper and cook until well done, stirring frequently. Combine tomatoes, tomato paste, water, milk, and Butter Buds and add to vegetables and turkey. Blend thoroughly. Cover and simmer for 45 minutes, stirring occasionally. Serve over cooked spaghetti. (Serves 6)

PER SERVING

Calories:	358
Fat:	3.2 grams
Cholesterol:	44 milligrams

🍒 Linguini with Smoked Salmon Sauce

This tasty dish of Linguini with Smoked Salmon Sauce intrigued me when I was first introduced to it by a notable television personality and cook show host. He was quick to point out the use of a heart-healthy ingredient, salmon, for this unusual pasta recipe.

The late 1980s made health-conscious adults aware of the merits associated with increased fish oil consumption. Since salmon is one variety of fish rich in omega-3 oils, its use on a regular basis in the daily diet is considered a healthy habit to develop. Therefore, the use of salmon in this unique dish seems to be a good choice. Well, look closely at the traditional version of this recipe before placing it into your healthy choice recipe file! Note the use of oil, butter, and heavy cream. Any benefit derived from the omega-3 oil (natural fish oil) of the salmon in this recipe is dramatically offset by the use of these high-fat ingredients.

When I revised the original recipe I tried to retain the rich flavor and creamy texture of this unusual pasta dish, without using fat-laden ingredients. I substituted a mixture of white wine and Butter Buds for the oil and butter. Evaporated skim milk replaces the heavy cream, because it offers a similar creamy texture without the fat and cholesterol. Additionally, I used defatted chicken broth instead of beef broth in an attempt to reduce fat content even more.

The revised version actually tastes better than the original, which I found excessively rich. Moreover, the low-fat version offers a more appropriate setting for the salmon—one that is in keeping with its reputation as a healthy food choice.

Traditional Recipe

- 2 tablespoons olive oil
- 3½ ounces smoked salmon
- 1 medium onion, chopped
- 2 cloves garlic, minced
- 2 scallions, chopped
- 1 green pepper, chopped
- 2 tablespoons butter
- 1 cup beef broth
- 1 cup crushed tomatoes in purée
- ½ cup heavy cream
- 1 pound linguini, cooked

Low-Fat Version

- 2 tablespoons white wine
  Butter Buds equivalent to 6 tablespoons butter
- 3½ ounces smoked salmon, chopped
- 1 medium onion, chopped
- 2 cloves garlic, minced
- 2 scallions, chopped
- 1 green pepper, chopped
- 1 cup defatted chicken broth
- 1 cup crushed tomatoes in purée
- ½ cup evaporated skim milk
- 1 pound linguini, cooked

In a large skillet, sauté salmon, onion, garlic, scallions, and green pepper for 5 minutes, stirring several times. Add butter and stir until melted and blended with other ingredients. Add beef broth and tomatoes and blend well. Simmer for 10 minutes. Stir in heavy cream and simmer another 1–2 minutes. Spoon sauce over platter of cooked linguini. (Serves 6)

PER SERVING

Calories:	408
Fat:	18.5 grams
Cholesterol:	50 milligrams

Dissolve dry Butter Buds in wine. Add to large, nonstick skillet and heat. Add salmon, onion, garlic, scallions, and green pepper. Sauté for 5 minutes, stirring several times. Add chicken broth and tomatoes and blend well. Simmer for 10 minutes. Stir in evaporated skim milk and simmer another 1–2 minutes. Spoon sauce over platter of cooked linguini. (Serves 6)

PER SERVING

Calories:	285
Fat:	2.6 grams
Cholesterol:	12 milligrams

Ziti with Broccoli and Bacon

The following traditional recipe for Ziti with Broccoli and Bacon can be converted into a healthier alternative by using turkey ham instead of bacon. Although the cholesterol content of bacon and turkey breast is the same, the fat content differs. It is important to look beyond just cholesterol content to assure a heart-healthy meal. We must focus on an even bigger culprit—FAT, especially the saturated variety. A comparison of the fat content of turkey versus bacon reveals a totally different scenario than that of cholesterol content. Turkey ham has slightly more than 1 gram of fat per ounce, while bacon totes a hefty 16 grams per ounce. Since a diet high in fat, particularly saturated fat, can trigger the body to produce more cholesterol, we must pay attention to both the cholesterol content and fat content of food.

In the revised recipe, replacing the bacon with turkey ham and eliminating the cooking oil nets a radical reduction in fat per serving and a healthier version of this terrific pasta dish. Moreover, it clearly demonstrates that reading labels for cholesterol content alone could prove hazardous to your health if you stop there! For a healthier you, always read on and check the fat content, as well. You may find that the item belongs back on the grocer's shelf, rather than in your grocery cart!

Traditional Recipe

4 tablespoons olive oil
2 cloves garlic, minced
3 cups fresh broccoli flowerettes
1 large red bell pepper, cut into strips
½ pound bacon strips, cooked and crumbled
8 ounces ziti macaroni, cooked

Ziti with Broccoli and Turkey Ham
Low-Fat Version

¼ cup rose wine
2 cloves garlic, minced
3 cups broccoli flowerettes Butter Buds equal to 4 tablespoons butter (undiluted)
1 to 2 tablespoons warm tap water
1 large red bell pepper, cut into strips
3 ounces lean turkey ham, thinly shaved and minced
2 drops liquid smoke flavoring (optional)
⅛ teaspoon crushed red pepper (optional)
8 ounces ziti macaroni, cooked

In a large skillet, sauté minced garlic in 3 tablespoons of olive oil until golden brown. Add broccoli flowerettes and cook over medium heat about 8–10 minutes until tender. With a slotted spoon, remove broccoli and garlic and set aside. Heat remaining tablespoon of olive oil in same skillet. Add red pepper strips and stir-fry over medium heat for 4–5 minutes. Return broccoli to skillet and sprinkle crumbled bacon over mixture. Toss to combine all ingredients. Cook for an additional 1–2 minutes, until well-heated. Combine cooked ziti and broccoli mixture in a large pasta bowl and toss until well-blended. (Serves 4)

Per Serving

Calories:	393
Fat:	24.5 grams
Cholesterol:	14 milligrams

Heat wine in large, nonstick skillet. Add garlic and broccoli and cook over medium heat about 8–10 minutes until broccoli is tender. With a slotted spoon, remove broccoli and set aside. In a small bowl or cup, combine dry Butter Buds with 1 or 2 tablespoons of warm water and blend to the consistency of melted butter. Add to skillet, along with red pepper strips and turkey ham. If desired, add liquid smoke flavoring and crushed pepper. Stir-fry pepper and ham for 4–5 minutes. Return broccoli to skillet and blend all ingredients thoroughly. Cook for an additional 1–2 minutes, until well-heated. Combine cooked ziti and broccoli mixture in large pasta bowl and toss until well-blended. (Serves 4)

Per Serving

Calories:	219
Fat:	2.1 grams
Cholesterol:	15 milligrams

Food for Thought

"I am a great eater of beef, and I believe it does harm to my wit."

—SHAKESPEARE (*Twelfth Night*)

"No one is lonely while eating spaghetti, it requires too much attention."

—CHRISTOPHER MORELY

VEGETARIAN PASTAS, ENTREES, AND SIDE DISHES

Pasta Caponata

Pasta Caponata, prepared in either of the two ways shown below, contains absolutely no cholesterol. However, the traditional recipe contains four times more fat than the low-fat version, mainly because of the oil used in the former recipe.

It is neither possible nor advisable to prepare a completely fat-free meal. The body needs a certain amount of fat to grow and develop. Furthermore, most foods, even foods such as fruits and vegetables that are not considered "fatty foods" by nature, contain small amounts of fat. For example, a medium-size apple contains about a half gram of fat. Thus, even when you think you are having a fat-free meal, those half grams here and there add up! Naturally, the fat in most fruits and vegetables is unsaturated, or "good fat." A daily diet that includes moderate portions of poultry and fish, along with generous amounts of complex carbohydrates, fruits, and vegetables contains a sufficient amount of "good fat" to serve the body's needs. Therefore, the use of added fat, such as oil and margarine, usually serves no good purpose. Added fat merely puts you over your daily fat allowance while piling on unnecessary calories.

With this in mind, I created the revised, low-fat version of Pasta Caponata. Notice that the only change in the recipe is the elimination of the oil and the subsequent elimination of about 9 grams of fat per serving. I don't know about you, but if I'm going to splurge on an extra dose of fat, it's going to be on something with a little more taste than cooking oil!

Traditional Recipe

¼ cup olive oil
2 cloves garlic, minced
1 large onion, chopped
1 medium eggplant, peeled and cubed
2 tablespoons capers, drained
2 tablespoons chopped fresh parsley
  salt and pepper to taste
1 28-ounce can crushed tomatoes in purée
1 6-ounce can tomato paste
2 cups water
1 pound ziti macaroni, cooked

Low-Fat Version

¼ cup white wine
2 cloves garlic, minced
1 large onion, chopped
1 medium eggplant, peeled and cubed
2 tablespoons capers, drained
2 tablespoons chopped fresh parsley
  salt and pepper to taste
1 28-ounce can crushed tomatoes in purée
1 6-ounce can tomato paste
2 cups water
1 pound ziti macaroni, cooked

In a large saucepan or Dutch oven, heat oil. Add garlic and onion and sauté until tender. Add cubed eggplant, capers, chopped parsley, salt, and pepper. Cook, uncovered, over medium heat for about 10 minutes. Add tomatoes, tomato paste, and water. Blend thoroughly. Cover and simmer for 45 minutes, stirring occasionally. Spoon sauce over cooked macaroni. (Serves 6)

PER SERVING

Calories: 360
Fat: 12 grams
Cholesterol: none

In a large saucepan or Dutch oven, heat wine. Add garlic and onion and sauté until tender. Add cubed eggplant, capers, chopped parsley, salt, and pepper. Cook, uncovered, over medium heat for about 10 minutes. Add tomatoes, tomato paste, and water. Blend thoroughly. Cover and simmer for 45 minutes, stirring occasionally. Spoon sauce over cooked macaroni. (Serves 6)

PER SERVING

Calories: 288
Fat: 3 grams
Cholesterol: none

Manicotti

One can hardly claim an Italian heritage without an occasional Sunday afternoon dinner of Manicotti. These cheese-filled delights are best when the shells are home-made; but, for those on the go, the boxed manicotti shells from the pasta aisle at the supermarket shorten the preparation time considerably.

The traditional version of this recipe was one of my mother-in-law's specialties. No one made it better. However, when I embarked on a mission of lowering fat and cholesterol intake, Mom's recipe had to undergo some surgery. The key changes involved substituting skim or low-fat dairy products for the whole milk ingredients in the recipe. In the revised version, skim milk and low-fat cottage cheese replace whole milk and ricotta cheese. Also, egg substitute is used instead of eggs. This substitution alone eliminates over 400 milligrams of cholesterol from the recipe. Since both the mozzarella and Parmesan cheeses are eliminated, some extra herbs and seasonings are added to compensate for the missing flavor in the filling. The low-fat manicotti is somewhat lighter and less filling than the original; but, when you consider the reduced calorie and fat content in each serving, you can treat yourself to a second helping and not feel guilty. Check the numbers at the end of each recipe if you need to be convinced.

Traditional Recipe

CRÊPES
1 cup flour
¼ teaspoon salt
1 egg
1 cup milk

FILLING
1 pound ricotta cheese
1 egg, slightly beaten
4 ounces shredded
   mozzarella cheese
¼ cup grated Parmesan
   cheese
2 tablespoons chopped
   parsley
salt and pepper to taste

TOMATO SAUCE
use 4 cups of meatless
   spaghetti sauce

Combine flour and salt and set aside. Place egg in medium mixing bowl and beat until frothy. Gradually add flour mixture and milk to eggs in alternating fashion, mixing thoroughly after each addition until batter is smooth (should be the consistency of pancake batter). Lightly grease and heat 7-inch crêpe pan or skillet. Pour in 2 or 3 tablespoons of batter, then lift pan above heating unit and tilt in all directions, allowing batter to coat bottom of pan. (This must be done quickly, before batter sets.) Return pan to heating unit and cook on medium heat until lightly brown on bottom and dry on top. Carefully loosen edges of crêpe and flip it over. Cook on opposite side for about 20 seconds. Remove crêpe from pan and place on paper towel to cool. Repeat until all batter has been used. (Makes about 12 crêpes.)

In a medium bowl, combine ricotta cheese and egg, mixing well. Add remaining ingredients and blend thoroughly. Place a crêpe on a plate and spoon filling along center of crêpe. Fold one side of crêpe over filling. Then fold over other side so it overlaps the first. Fill remaining crêpes in same manner.

Place a small amount of tomato sauce in bottom of large, rectangular baking pan. Arrange filled manicotti side by side in pan. Top with additional tomato sauce and bake at 350° for 35–40 minutes. (Serves 4)

PER SERVING

Calories:	589
Fat:	29 grams
Cholesterol:	205 milligrams

Manicotti (continued)

Low-Fat Version

CRÊPES
 1 cup flour
 ¼ teaspoon salt
   non-cholesterol egg
     substitute equal to 1 egg
 1 cup skim milk

FILLING
 1 pound low-fat cottage
     cheese (1% or less)
   non-cholesterol egg
     substitute equal to 1 egg
 ½ teaspoon dried basil
 ¼ teaspoon garlic powder
 ⅛ teaspoon ground cloves
 2 tablespoons chopped
     parsley
   salt and pepper to taste

TOMATO SAUCE
   use 4 cups of meatless
     spaghetti sauce

Combine flour and salt and set aside. Place egg substitute in medium mixing bowl and beat. Gradually add flour mixture and milk to egg substitute in alternating fashion, mixing thoroughly after each addition until batter is smooth (should be consistency of pancake batter). Heat 7-inch crêpe pan or nonstick skillet. Pour in 2 tablespoons of batter, then lift pan above heating unit and tilt in all directions, allowing batter to coat bottom of pan. (This must be done quickly, before batter sets.) Return pan to heating unit and cook on medium heat until lightly brown on bottom and dry on top. Carefully loosen edges of crêpe and flip it over. Cook on opposite side for about 20 seconds. Remove crêpe from pan and place on paper towel to cool. Repeat until all batter is used. (Makes about 12 crêpes.)

In a medium bowl, combine cottage cheese and egg substitute. Add all other filling ingredients and blend thoroughly. Place a crêpe on a plate and spoon filling along center of crêpe. Fold one side of crêpe over filling. Then fold over other side so it overlaps the first. Fill remaining crêpes in same manner.

Place a small amount of tomato sauce in bottom of large, rectangular baking pan. Arrange filled manicotti side by side in pan. Top with additional tomato sauce and bake at 350° for 35–40 minutes. (Serves 4)

Per Serving

Calories:	297
Fat:	1 gram
Cholesterol:	7 milligrams

Spinach-Stuffed Shells

When compared to high-fat, high-cholesterol meat dishes, Spinach-Stuffed Shells, even in its original version, is an acceptable meal for health-conscious individuals striving to reduce the amount of fat and cholesterol in their diet. However, with a few simple substitutions, this tasty Italian dish can be modified to reflect even lower values with regard to calories, fat, and cholesterol. I obtained these reductions by replacing the whole milk dairy products (cheese, milk) with low-fat versions and by using egg substitute in place of whole egg. These substitutions result in a significant decrease in fat and cholesterol, along with a reduction of about 130 calories per serving. There is almost no taste difference between the two versions.

Traditional Recipe

1 package frozen spinach (10 ounces)
¼ cup chopped scallions
12 ounces ricotta cheese (whole milk type)
1 egg
¼ cup whole milk (optional)
¼ cup chopped fresh parsley
½ teaspoon salt (or to taste)
¼ teaspoon pepper
¼ teaspoon garlic powder
20 large pasta shells
4 cups meatless spaghetti sauce

Low-Fat Version

1 package frozen spinach (10 ounces)
¼ cup chopped scallions
12 ounces low-fat cottage cheese (1% or less)
egg substitute equivalent to 1 egg
¼ cup skim milk (optional)
¼ cup chopped fresh parsley
½ teaspoon salt (or to taste)
¼ teaspoon pepper
¼ teaspoon garlic powder
20 large pasta shells
4 cups meatless spaghetti sauce

Cook spinach and scallions in a small amount of water, following instructions on spinach package. Drain. Mix ricotta cheese, egg, milk (if necessary to thin), and parsley in medium bowl. Add spinach and onion mixture along with salt, pepper, and garlic powder. Mix thoroughly. Partially boil pasta shells (about 9 minutes) and stuff with spinach and cheese filling. Spread about 1 cup of spaghetti sauce on bottom of baking dish. Arrange shells in dish and top with remaining 3 cups of spaghetti sauce. Cover and bake at 350° for 30 minutes. (Serves 4)

PER SERVING

Calories:	420
Fat:	15.6 grams
Cholesterol:	100 milligrams

Cook spinach and scallions in small amount of water, following the instructions on the spinach package. Drain. Mix cottage cheese, egg substitute, milk (if necessary to thin), and parsley in medium bowl. Add spinach and onion mixture along with salt, pepper, and garlic powder. Mix thoroughly. Partially boil pasta shells (about 9 minutes) and stuff with spinach and cheese filling. Spread about 1 cup of spaghetti sauce on bottom of baking dish. Arrange shells in dish and top with remaining 3 cups of spaghetti sauce. Cover and bake at 350° for 30 minutes. (Serves 4)

PER SERVING

Calories:	290
Fat:	1.9 grams
Cholesterol:	5 milligrams

🍒 Pasta Primavera al Diavolo

Here is a great vegetable dish that is relatively low in saturated fat and cholesterol even when prepared according to the original recipe. However, with a few minor adjustments, the calories and total fat content are reduced even further in the revised version.

As with many recipes, the ingredients that add calories and fat are oil and butter. Even using the purest, lightest, virgin olive oil and the finest grade of liquid vegetable oil or margarine doesn't change the total picture much. Although the use of margarine instead of butter reduces cholesterol content, it does not reduce total fat. Vegetable oil and margarine contain as much fat as butter and other solid shortenings, such as lard. So if your goal is reduction of total fat, these ingredients must go—or, at least, be limited.

In the Pasta Primavera al Diavolo recipe that follows, the oil adds little in terms of taste because the vegetables take over and dictate the flavor. In fact, the use of wine in the low-fat version in place of the oil actually enhances the taste. This improvement is especially evident if a semi-dry white wine with a fruity flavor, such as Muscatel, is used. Additionally, the elimination of butter doesn't diminish the flavor a bit because Butter Buds is used in its place to provide the necessary butter flavor. The bonus associated with omitting the butter and oil is clearly shown by a comparison of the fat content of each version of the recipe below.

Traditional Recipe

2 tablespoons olive oil
3 tablespoons butter
1 medium zucchini, diced (about 2 cups)
1 cup chopped onions
1 carrot, finely chopped
1 large green pepper, diced
6 small fresh plum tomatoes, chopped
¼ cup chopped fresh parsley
⅛ teaspoon cayenne pepper (optional)
salt to taste (optional)
1 pound spaghetti, cooked

Low-Fat Version

Butter Buds equivalent to 4 tablespoons butter
¼ cup semi-dry white wine (Muscatel)
1 medium zucchini, diced (about 2 cups)
1 cup chopped onions
1 carrot, finely chopped
1 large green pepper, diced
6 small fresh plum tomatoes, chopped
¼ cup chopped fresh parsley
⅛ teaspoon cayenne pepper (optional)
salt to taste (optional)
1 pound spaghetti, cooked

Combine olive oil and butter in large skillet and heat over medium-high heat until butter is melted. Add zucchini, onions, carrots, and green peppers and stir-fry over medium heat for about 4–5 minutes. Add tomatoes, parsley, and seasonings. Blend, cover, and simmer until vegetables are tender. If juices evaporate, add a small amount of water to prevent sticking. Spoon vegetable sauce over cooked pasta. (Serves 6)

PER SERVING

Calories:	345
Fat:	12 grams
Cholesterol:	18 milligrams

Dissolve Butter Buds in wine and heat in a large, nonstick skillet. Add zucchini, onions, carrots, and green peppers and stir-fry over medium heat for about 4–5 minutes. Add tomatoes, parsley, and seasonings. Blend, cover, and simmer until vegetables are tender. If juices evaporate, add a small amount of water to prevent sticking. Spoon vegetable sauce over cooked pasta. (Serves 6)

PER SERVING

Calories:	255
Fat:	1 gram
Cholesterol:	none

🦋 Pasta with Zucchini and Fresh Tomatoes

Pasta with Zucchini and Fresh Tomatoes is a great dish any time of the year, but I find it especially delicious during the summer months when home grown zucchini, tomatoes, and fresh herbs are plentiful and at their peak in flavor. With a large garden salad and crisp french bread, it's a quick and easy vegetarian meal. For heartier appetites, the pasta may be served as a side dish with a poultry or fish entrée.

Prepared in the traditional manner, olive oil is used for sautéing and stir-frying the vegetables. Additionally, the finished product is sprinkled with Parmesan cheese. In the revised, low-fat version, white wine replaces olive oil and the cheese is eliminated. To make up for the absence of the cheese, I use a little extra salt. The Parmesan cheese in the original recipe contains almost 200 milligrams of sodium, so you can afford an extra dash of salt as a replacement. These minor changes result in a modest drop in calories and a significant reduction in fat content per serving. Admittedly, the original recipe using the olive oil and Parmesan cheese is wonderful, but every time I am tempted to prepare it that way, I remind myself that my revised, low-fat version has one tenth the fat.

Traditional Recipe

3 medium zucchini, pared and cubed (about 1 pound)
2 tablespoons lemon juice
¼ cup olive oil
3 cloves garlic, minced
2 medium onions, sliced and separated into rings
3 large ripe tomatoes, thinly sliced
¼ cup chopped fresh basil
1 tablespoon chopped fresh parsley
½ teaspoon crushed red pepper
¼ teaspoon salt
2 tablespoons grated Parmesan cheese
1 pound ziti macaroni, cooked

Low-Fat Version

3 medium zucchini, pared and cubed (about 1 pound)
2 tablespoons lemon juice
¼ cup white semi-dry wine
3 cloves garlic, minced
2 medium onions, sliced and separated into rings
3 large ripe tomatoes, thinly sliced
¼ cup chopped fresh basil
1 tablespoon chopped fresh parsley
½ teaspoon crushed red pepper
salt to taste (optional)
1 pound ziti macaroni, cooked

Toss zucchini with lemon juice and set aside. In a large skillet, heat oil. Add minced garlic and sauté until golden brown. Add zucchini and onions, and stir-fry for 3–4 minutes. Add tomatoes, basil, parsley, red pepper, and salt. Toss to blend ingredients. Cover skillet, reduce heat, and simmer until zucchini is tender. Sprinkle with cheese and toss lightly. Arrange cooked ziti in large oval platter or pasta bowl. Spoon zucchini mixture over pasta and serve immediately. (Serves 6)

PER SERVING

Calories:	333
Fat:	10.6 grams
Cholesterol:	1 milligram

Toss zucchini with lemon juice and set aside. In a large, nonstick skillet, sauté minced garlic in wine over high heat for about 1 minute. Add zucchini and onions, and stir-fry for 3–4 minutes. Add tomatoes, basil, parsley, red pepper, and salt (if desired). Toss several times to blend ingredients. Cover skillet, reduce heat, and simmer until zucchini is tender. Arrange cooked ziti in large oval platter or pasta bowl. Spoon zucchini mixture over pasta and serve immediately. (Serves 6)

PER SERVING

Calories:	275
Fat:	1 gram
Cholesterol:	none

Eggplant Parmesan

Eggplant Parmesan has always been one of my favorite Italian meals. However, after embarking on a low-fat, low-cholesterol mission, I soon realized that this dish, prepared in the traditional manner with rich cheeses and olive oil, would either have to go or be modified to accommodate my new life style.

The culprits in the traditional version are the oil, cheese, and eggs. The oil and cheese contribute to the high-fat content, thus increasing the calories per serving; while the use of whole eggs increases the cholesterol content significantly.

In the modified version, the eggs used to help coat the eggplant are eliminated. Natural moisture from the eggplant is sufficient to allow bread crumbs to adhere. In fact, a smaller quantity of crumbs is needed when the egg dip is eliminated. In addition, low-fat cottage cheese replaces the mozzarella and Parmesan cheeses in the revised recipe. Finally, the eggplant is breaded and broiled, rather than fried. Compare the calorie, fat, and cholesterol content of each version.

Traditional Recipe

1 medium eggplant (about 1 pound)
1 cup bread crumbs
½ teaspoon salt
¼ teaspoon pepper
½ teaspoon garlic powder
½ teaspoon oregano
2 eggs
½ cup olive oil
1 cup chopped onions
2 cups crushed tomatoes
8 ounces shredded mozzarella cheese
½ cup grated Parmesan cheese

Low-Fat Version

1 medium eggplant (about 1 pound)
3 tablespoons fine cracker crumbs or nonfat bread crumbs
½ teaspoon salt
¼ teaspoon pepper
½ teaspoon garlic powder
½ teaspoon oregano
1 cup chopped onions
2 cups crushed tomatoes
1 cup dry-curd cottage cheese (1% or less)

Peel eggplant and cut into ³/₈-inch-thick slices. Combine bread crumbs, salt, pepper, garlic powder, and oregano. Dip eggplant slices into beaten eggs and then press into bread crumb mixture, coating each slice thoroughly. Set aside. In a medium saucepan sauté onions until tender in 1 tablespoon of the olive oil. Add crushed tomatoes. Cover and simmer for about 10 minutes. In the meantime, pour remaining olive oil into large frying pan and heat. Place breaded eggplant slices into hot oil and fry until golden brown (about 3–4 minutes on each side). Remove eggplant from frying pan and place on paper towel to drain excess oil. Next, place 2 or 3 tablespoons of tomato sauce on bottom of 9 × 13-inch baking dish. Arrange layer of eggplant slices on top of sauce. Spread a layer of mozzarella over eggplant. Then top with additional sauce and sprinkle with Parmesan cheese. Repeat layers until all ingredients are used up ending with tomato sauce topped with Parmesan cheese. Cover with aluminum foil and bake at 375° for 30 minutes. (Serves 6)

Per Serving

Calories:	474
Fat:	30 grams
Cholesterol:	111 milligrams

Peel eggplant and cut into ³/₈-inch-thick slices. Combine cracker or bread crumbs, salt, pepper, garlic powder, and oregano. Press eggplant slices into crumb mixture, coating each slice thoroughly. Arrange slices on cookie sheet in single layer. Broil 6–7 minutes on each side to brown. While eggplant is broiling, dry-sauté onions until tender in medium, nonstick saucepan. Add tomatoes. Cover and simmer for 10 minutes. Place 2 or 3 tablespoons of tomato sauce on the bottom of a 9 × 13-inch baking dish. Arrange layer of eggplant slices on top of sauce. Place a small amount of cottage cheese on each eggplant slice; then top with additional sauce. Repeat layers until all ingredients are used up, ending with tomato sauce layer. Cover with aluminum foil and bake at 375° for 30 minutes. (Serves 6)

Per Serving

Calories:	90
Fat:	0.4 grams
Cholesterol:	2 milligrams

Stir-Fry Vegetable Medley

There are a few regulars that always appear on my party buffet table. One of these is a tray of fresh vegetables and dip (made with my low-fat sour cream, of course!). When the party's over, I generally end up with an assortment of leftover fresh vegetables, each variety in its own little plastic bag in the crisper section of my refrigerator. Usually there's not enough of any one vegetable to use for a meal, so a stir-fry vegetable medley seems a reasonable solution for an overcrowded vegetable crisper! This Vegetable Stir-Fry Medley makes a delightful vegetable accompaniment to a chicken or fish entrée. Or, if you prefer, cut up some leftover cooked chicken or turkey, add to the fried vegetables, and serve over cooked brown rice for a complete meal.

Below are two versions of the Vegetable Stir-Fry Medley recipe. Though I've listed only broccoli and cauliflower for ingredients, almost any assortment of fresh vegetables works well. The important difference in the two versions is the fat content. In the traditional recipe, the vegetables are stir-fried in oil, and butter is added for flavoring. The revised recipe uses pineapple juice instead of oil and Butter Buds instead of butter for flavoring.

You'll discover that the stir-fry using juice instead of oil actually tastes better! The vegetables remain crisp and crunchy, instead of limp and soggy. So, next time you have leftover fresh vegetables, try stir-frying them according to the low-fat recipe below. Adding unnecessary fat to a nutritious vegetable dish is about as senseless as adding 500 calories of salad dressing to a dieter's salad plate!

Traditional Recipe

2 tablespoons peanut oil
2 cups broccoli flowerettes
2 cups cauliflower flowerettes
1 tablespoon melted butter
2 tablespoons pineapple juice
1/2 teaspoon onion powder
dash or 2 soy sauce
2 tablespoons crushed pineapple

Low-Fat Version

4 tablespoons pineapple juice
2 cups broccoli flowerettes
2 cups cauliflower flowerettes
Butter Buds equivalent to 2 tablespoons butter
1/2 teaspoon onion powder
dash or 2 soy sauce
2 tablespoons crushed pineapple

In a wok or large skillet, heat oil until very hot. Add broccoli and cauliflower and stir-fry for 1 minute on high heat. Add melted butter, pineapple juice, onion powder, soy sauce and continue stir-frying for several minutes until vegetables are done to the crisp-tender stage, or to your likeness. Add crushed pineapple and toss gently for another minute. Serve as a side dish with poultry or fish. (Serves 4)

Per Serving

Calories: 124
Fat: 10.2 grams
Cholesterol: 9 milligrams

In a nonstick wok or large skillet, heat pineapple juice to bubbling. Add broccoli and cauliflower and toss to coat with juice. Add Butter Buds, onion powder, and soy sauce and stir-fry on high heat for several minutes until vegetables are done to the crisp-tender stage, or to your likeness. (Do not overcook.) Add crushed pineapple and toss gently for another minute. Serve as a side dish with poultry or fish. (Serves 4)

Per Serving

Calories: 45
Fat: less than 1 gram
Cholesterol: none

 **Polynesian Rice**

Here is a quick, delicious dish for rice lovers. Polynesian Rice can be served alone as a light meal, or as a side dish with fish or poultry. Either way, you will enjoy the south sea flavor of this combination of ingredients.

Typically, the recipe uses tuna in oil, adding unnecessary fat and calories to each serving. Thus, water-packed tuna is substituted in the revised recipe.

The second change, using pineapple packed in juice rather than in heavy syrup, does little to alter fat content; however, it eliminates unnecessary sugar, thereby reducing calories. Since weight control is an important aspect of a heart-healthy life style, eliminating unnecessary calories, when possible, makes sense.

A final revision incorporates brown rice as the replacement for the ordinary white rice used in the original recipe. Because brown rice retains its bran coat, it enhances the nutritional value of this dish by adding fiber along with many important vitamins and minerals that are often lacking in polished white rice. Although the original recipe is not nutritionally bad, the revisions make the low-fat version of Polynesian Rice even healthier.

Traditional Recipe

1 6½-ounce can tuna in oil, drained
1 cup pineapple tidbits in syrup
2 cups cooked rice
1 tablespoon soy sauce
1 4-ounce can sliced mushrooms, drained
¼ cup finely minced scallions

Low-Fat Version

1 6½-ounce can water-packed tuna, drained
1 cup pineapple tidbits in juice
2 cups cooked brown rice
1 tablespoon soy sauce
1 4-ounce can sliced mushrooms, drained
¼ cup finely minced scallions

In a large bowl, combine tuna and undrained pineapple. Add cooked rice, soy sauce, mushrooms, and scallions. Toss until well-blended. Spoon into ovenproof casserole and bake uncovered at 325° for 1 hour. (Serves 6)

Per Serving

Calories:	185
Fat:	3 grams
Cholesterol:	27 milligrams

In a large bowl, combine tuna and pineapple in juice. Add cooked rice, soy sauce, mushrooms, and scallions. Toss until well-blended. Spoon into a nonstick ovenproof casserole and bake, uncovered, at 325° for 45 minutes. (Serves 6)

Per Serving

Calories:	138
Fat:	0.2 gram
Cholesterol:	19 milligrams

Apple-Bread Stuffing

There is something about cold weather that calls for stuffing instead of potato. With or without the turkey, a casserole of stuffing will complement almost any poultry or fish entrée.

One of my family's favorite stuffings is Apple-Bread Stuffing. It has been in my recipe file for years and has undergone revision twice. The original recipe called for an egg and butter. In an effort to reduce the cholesterol content of the recipe, I eliminated the egg and substituted margarine for the butter. (Egg whites could have been used in place of the whole egg, but since the recipe worked well without either, I eliminated both.) These changes reduced the cholesterol in the recipe, but did nothing to reduce the fat, since margarine contains as much fat as butter.

Recently, I revamped the recipe again, this time concentrating on fat. I substituted Butter Buds for margarine, which reduced the fat per serving by about 10 grams and cut the calorie content in half. I made the low-fat version for ten guests at a holiday dinner party and they all raved about it.

Traditional Recipe

2³/₄ cups water
1 chicken bouillon cube
¹/₂ cup butter
1 cup chopped celery
1 cup chopped onions
4 cups toasted bread cubes
   or stuffing mix
   salt and pepper to taste
¹/₂ teaspoon sage
2 cups diced apples

Low-Fat Version

2³/₄ cups water
1 chicken bouillon cube
   Butter Buds equivalent to
   ¹/₂ cup butter
1 cup chopped celery
1 cup chopped onions
4 cups whole-wheat bread
   crumbs (made from
   nonfat bread such as
   pita bread)
   salt and pepper to taste
¹/₂ teaspoon sage
2 cups diced apples

Boil water. Add bouillon cube, butter, celery, and onions. Simmer 5 minutes. Add bread cubes and toss until all liquid is absorbed. Season with salt, pepper, and sage. Add apples and mix thoroughly. Spoon stuffing into a lightly greased 2-quart casserole. Cover and bake at 350° for 45 minutes. Remove cover and bake an additional 15 minutes to brown lightly. (Serves 10)

PER SERVING

Calories:	183
Fat:	10.6 grams
Cholesterol:	29 milligrams

Boil water. Add bouillon cube, Butter Buds, celery, and onions. Simmer 5 minutes. Add bread crumbs and toss until all liquid is absorbed. Season with salt, pepper, and sage. Add apples and mix thoroughly. Spoon stuffing into a 2-quart, nonstick casserole. Cover and bake at 350° for 45 minutes. Remove cover and bake an additional 15 minutes to brown lightly. (Serves 10)

PER SERVING

Calories:	95
Fat:	less than 1 gram
Cholesterol:	none

Waldorf Salad

Refreshing, light, and low calorie are words commonly used to describe fresh fruit and vegetable salads. But those adjectives can become meaningless the minute we spoon on that dollop of salad dressing. The classic Waldorf Salad, prepared in the traditional way, is a perfect example. It begins with firm, juicy apple chunks and crisp celery; but by the time we've added chopped nuts and mayonnaise, we've turned this seemingly light fruit salad into a fat-laden nemesis. What are the alternatives for someone who enjoys waldorf salad? With some recipe modification you can have the best of both worlds—this classic favorite, in low-fat form!

In the traditional recipe walnuts and mayonnaise each contribute equally to the high-fat content of the Waldorf Salad. In the revised version, raisins replace walnuts and nonfat yogurt is used instead of mayonnaise. I think you'll find the reduction in calories and fat content well worth the trade-off.

Traditional Recipe

1½ cups chopped apples
1 cup chopped celery
½ cup chopped walnuts
½ teaspoon lemon juice
¼ cup mayonnaise
1 tablespoon sugar
  outer leaves of head of
  lettuce (optional)

Low-Fat Version

1½ cups chopped apples
1 cup chopped celery
½ cup dark raisins
½ teaspoon lemon juice
⅓ cup nonfat plain yogurt
1 teaspoon sugar
  outer leaves of head of
  lettuce (optional)

In a medium bowl combine apples, celery, and walnuts. Sprinkle with lemon juice and toss. Combine mayonnaise and sugar and add to apple mixture. Toss again until well-blended. Serve on beds of lettuce on individual salad plates. (Serves 4)

Per Serving

Calories:	240
Fat:	20.9 grams
Cholesterol:	9 milligrams

In a medium bowl combine apples, celery, and raisins. Sprinkle with lemon juice and toss. Combine yogurt and sugar and add to apple mixture. Toss again until well-blended. Serve on beds of lettuce on individual salad plates. (Serves 4)

Per Serving

Calories:	95
Fat:	0.5 gram
Cholesterol:	0.3 milligram

Food for Thought

"Tomatoes and oregano make it Italian.
Wine and tarragon make it French.
Sour Cream makes it Russian.
Lemon and cinnamon make it Greek.
Soy sauce makes it Chinese.
Garlic makes it good."
—ALICE MAY BROCK
(Alice's Restaurant)

POULTRY, FISH, AND MEAT DISHES

🍒 *Zesty Chicken with Rice*

This Zesty Chicken with Rice dinner has been revised to fit the needs of those counting calories, as well as grams of fat. It also provides a classic example of "hidden fat overdose" from a food source that most of us use daily—ordinary salad dressing.

Prepared in the traditional way, this chicken dinner uses bottled Italian salad dressing, which causes the fat content to soar. However, in the revised recipe, I have substituted an oil-free Italian salad dressing. This alteration cuts the calories per serving almost in half.

If you absolutely cannot find an oil-free dressing, a lite dressing may be used. Check the label, however, and make certain that it contains less than 7 calories per tablespoon. The standard Italian dressing averages close to 90 calories per tablespoon, most of which are "fat" calories from the large quantity of oil in the dressing. Keep in mind, also, that a tablespoon of salad dressing does not go very far. It should come as no surprise, therefore, that some people believe they are dieting when eating at salad bars only to find that even with their best efforts, instead of losing weight, they've gained! They forgot about the fattening oils in salad dressings.

Traditional Recipe

- 4 boneless chicken breast halves
- ⅓ cup Italian salad dressing
- ⅔ cup uncooked minute rice
- 1 bag frozen broccoli, carrots, water chestnuts, and red pepper combo (Green Giant Fanfare)
- 1¾ cups chicken bouillon
- ½ teaspoon Italian herb seasoning

Low-Fat Version

- 4 boneless chicken breast halves
- ⅓ cup Italian oil-free salad dressing
- ⅔ cup uncooked minute rice
- 1 bag frozen broccoli, carrots, water chestnuts, and red pepper combo (Green Giant Fanfare)
- 1¾ cups seasoned defatted chicken broth
- ½ teaspoon Italian herb seasoning

Preheat oven to 400°. Arrange chicken in 9 × 12-inch baking pan. Pour salad dressing over chicken. Bake uncovered for 20 minutes. Place rice under and around chicken, and surround with mixed vegetables. Combine bouillon and Italian herb seasoning. Pour over chicken and vegetables. Cover and bake for 25 minutes more. (Serves 4)

Per Serving

Calories: 426
Fat: 27 grams
Cholesterol: 66 milligrams

Preheat oven to 400°. Arrange chicken in 9 × 12-inch baking pan. Pour salad dressing over chicken. Bake uncovered for 20 minutes. Place rice under and around chicken, and surround with mixed vegetables. Combine chicken broth and Italian herb seasoning. Pour over chicken and vegetables. Cover and bake for 25 minutes longer. (Serves 4)

Per Serving

Calories: 220
Fat: 3.1 grams
Cholesterol: 66 milligrams

🐛 *Sausage Kabobs*

The word sausage automatically evokes a negative thought for those on a low-fat diet. Recently, however, I found some turkey sausage that was rather lean by comparison to the regular pork sausage and other brands of turkey sausage. Although I try to select foods that derive less than 20 percent of their calories from fat, and even this lean turkey sausage surpassed that amount somewhat, on rare occasions, I treat my family to a sausage meal. If you have a good butcher ask him to make it for you according to your specifications, with minimal fat and no skin. Remember to go easy on other fatty foods the day you're planning a turkey sausage dinner. The two versions of Sausage Kabobs are identical except for the choice of meat. One uses regular pork sausage and the other uses lean turkey sausage. You will notice that the pork sausage has more than twice the amount of fat as the turkey sausage, making it totally unacceptable for a heart-healthy diet. I suggest that if you have a burning desire for sausage, satisfy it occasionally; and then, only with extra lean turkey sausage. Remember, even the lean varieties contain generous amounts of fat, so keep the portions small!

Traditional Recipe

1 pound pork sausage
4 large Granny Smith apples
1 16-ounce can pineapple chunks in juice (drain and reserve juice)
4 tablespoons all fruit pineapple low-calorie spread or preserves

Low-Fat Version

1 pound turkey sausage
4 large Granny Smith apples
1 16-ounce can pineapple chunks in juice (drain and reserve juice)
4 tablespoons all fruit pineapple low-calorie spread or preserves

Place sausage in large skillet, cover with water, and bring to a boil. Reduce heat and simmer for 20 minutes. Remove sausage from skillet and drain on paper towel for several minutes. Next, place sausage on cutting surface and slice into ³/₄-inch-wide pieces. Set aside. Pare and core apples. Cut into quarters; and then cut each quarter in half, crosswise. Thread apples, sausage, and pineapple chunks onto six 12-inch skewers. Place preserves in small saucepan and heat. Add a tablespoon or two of reserved pineapple juice to thin, if necessary. Place kabobs on broiler pan; then, using a pastry brush, baste kabobs with preserves. Broil about 5 inches from heating unit for about 15 minutes, or until sausage is brown. Turn occasionally and brush with preserves. (Serves 6)

Per Serving

Calories:	295
Fat:	16.8 grams
Cholesterol:	40 milligrams

Place sausage in large skillet, cover with water, and bring to a boil. Reduce heat and simmer for about 20 minutes. Remove sausage from skillet and drain on paper towel for several minutes. Next, place sausage on cutting surface and slice into ³/₄-inch pieces. Set aside. Pare and core apples. Cut into quarters; and then cut each quarter in half, crosswise. Thread apples, sausage, and pineapple chunks onto six 12-inch skewers. Place preserves in small saucepan and heat. Add a tablespoon or two of reserved pineapple juice to thin, if necessary. Place kabobs on broiler pan; then, using a pastry brush, baste kabobs with preserves. Broil about 5 inches from heating unit for about 15 minutes, or until sausage is brown. Turn occasionally and brush with preserves. (Serves 6)

Per Serving

Calories:	210
Fat:	7.4 grams
Cholesterol:	34 milligrams

Swiss Steak

For years Americans have been bombarded with information on cholesterol and fat, along with the potential hazards associated with an excess of each in the daily diet. Unfortunately, much of what we hear and read is confusing and contradictory. But, there are some recommendations that seem constant and are rarely disputed by the health experts. Most health authorities suggest that we reduce the saturated fat in our diet by eating poultry and fish instead of red meat. For most of us, the elimination of red meat poses few problems. But for others, saying goodbye to some favorite red meat recipes may be a real sacrifice. Fortunately, not all red meat recipes must be made exclusively with red meat. Look at the two recipes for Swiss Steak. The revised version uses turkey breast instead of round steak. It is one way to reduce the saturated fat in your diet and still capture some of the spicy flavor of an old favorite. Make no mistake, however; it is still turkey, not beef! When you prepare the low-fat version for your family, please don't apologize for the absence of beef. You may even discover that they prefer it that way.

Traditional Recipe

¼ cup flour
    salt and pepper to taste
1½ pounds round steak
    (about ¾-inch thick)
3 tablespoons vegetable oil
½ cup chopped onions
1 16-ounce can plum
    tomatoes, chopped
¼ cup chopped green
    pepper

Swiss Turkey Steak Low-Fat Version

¼ cup flour
    salt and pepper, if
    desired
1½ pounds boneless turkey
    breast cutlet (about
    ¾-inch thick)
3 tablespoons white wine
½ cup chopped onions
1 16-ounce can plum
    tomatoes, chopped
¼ cup chopped green
    pepper

Combine flour, salt, and pepper; pound into meat with a meat mallet, working the seasoned flour into the steak. In a large skillet, heat oil. Add meat and brown on both sides. Add chopped onions and tomatoes. Cover and cook over low heat for about 1½ hours, or until steak is tender. Add green pepper and cook for an additional 15 minutes. Season to taste. (Serves 6)

PER SERVING

Calories: 318
Fat: 13.5 grams
Cholesterol: 81 milligrams

Combine flour, salt, and pepper; pound into turkey with a meat mallet, working the seasoned flour into the turkey. In a large, nonstick skillet, dry-sauté floured turkey breast over high heat until brown; turn and brown on opposite side. Add wine and tilt pan in all directions, so as to deglaze or loosen any flour residue that is adhering to the pan. Top with onions and tomatoes. Cover and cook over low heat for about 1 hour, or until turkey is tender. Add green pepper and cook for an additional 15 minutes. (Serves 6)

PER SERVING

Calories: 257
Fat: 3.5 grams
Cholesterol: 68 milligrams

Oriental Pork Stir-Fry

In our house, if there's not an Italian specialty simmering on the stove, there is usually an assortment of sliced goodies in bowls on the countertop, each item awaiting its turn in the wok. Stir-fry meals rank high on the list of favorites, second only to Italian. We stir-fry all year, especially during the summer months, when fresh vegetables are plentiful. The wok and the outdoor gas grill make a perfect duo for warm weather cookery. Most people will admit that spending hours in a hot kitchen on a summer day is not much fun. Stir-frying is an easy way to make quick meals and spend less time in the kitchen. The wok is the ideal kitchen aid for stir-frying; but, if you don't have one, a large skillet works almost as well.

Since my family enjoys stir-fry meals, I always look for new recipes. Except for the liberal use of oil, many stir-fry recipes are inherently low in fat and cholesterol, because most use small quantities of meat and an abundance of fresh vegetables. Even when a recipe calls for red meat, fish or poultry easily can be substituted and provides another way to reduce fat and cholesterol even further.

The following Oriental Pork Stir-Fry recipe lends itself well to conversion. The revised recipe for Oriental Chicken Stir-Fry preserves all of the spice and zest of the original, without the forbidden ingredients. Moreover, a comparison of the nutrient values at the end of each recipe makes a most convincing case for including the revised version in your recipe file!

Traditional Recipe

¾ pound thinly sliced pork tenderloin cutlets
2 tablespoons peanut oil
6 scallions, cut into 1-inch pieces
1 cup thinly sliced carrots
2 cups cauliflower flowerettes
2 cups broccoli flowerettes
1 8-ounce can sliced water chestnuts (drained)
½ cup chicken broth
1 teaspoon soy sauce
1 tablespoon cornstarch
1 tablespoon brown sugar
¼ teaspoon garlic powder
salt and pepper to taste

Oriental Chicken Stir-Fry Low-Fat Version

¾ pound thinly sliced chicken breast cutlets
2 tablespoons pineapple juice
6 scallions, cut into 1-inch pieces
1 cup thinly sliced carrots
2 cups cauliflower flowerettes
2 cups broccoli flowerettes
1 8-ounce can sliced water chestnuts (drained)
½ cup defatted chicken broth
1 teaspoon soy sauce
1 tablespoon cornstarch
1 tablespoon brown sugar
¼ teaspoon garlic powder
salt and pepper to taste

Cut pork into strips (about ³/₈-inch × 2 inches) and set aside. Heat 1 tablespoon of oil in large skillet or wok. Starting with scallions, add vegetables one at a time to the skillet, stir-frying for 1 minute after each addition. After last vegetable is added, continue stir-frying for another 3 or 4 minutes, until vegetables are cooked to the crisp-tender stage. Do not overcook. Remove vegetables from skillet and set aside. Add another tablespoon of oil to the skillet and stir-fry pork for 4 or 5 minutes, or until cooked. In a small bowl, combine chicken broth, soy sauce, cornstarch, brown sugar, and garlic powder. Blend well and add to pork. Stir over medium heat until mixture bubbles and thickens. Then, stir in vegetables and toss until all ingredients are heated. Season to taste with salt and pepper. (Serves 4)

PER SERVING

Calories:	353
Fat:	19.9 grams
Cholesterol:	75 milligrams

Cut chicken into strips (about ³/₈-inch × 2 inches) and set aside. Heat 1 tablespoon pineapple juice in large, nonstick skillet or wok. Starting with scallions, add vegetables one at a time to the skillet, stir-frying for 1 minute after each addition. After last vegetable is added, continue stir-frying for another 3 or 4 minutes, or until vegetables are cooked to the crisp-tender stage. Do not overcook. Remove vegetables from skillet and set aside. Add another tablespoon of pineapple juice to the skillet and stir-fry chicken for 3 or 4 minutes, or until cooked. In a small bowl, combine chicken broth, soy sauce, cornstarch, brown sugar, and garlic powder. Blend well and add to chicken. Stir over medium heat until mixture bubbles and thickens. Then, stir in vegetables and toss until all ingredients are heated. Season to taste with salt and pepper, if desired. (Serves 4)

PER SERVING

Calories:	237
Fat:	4.7 grams
Cholesterol:	66 milligrams

Cutlets with Sun-Dried Tomatoes

About a year ago, I convinced the chef of a gourmet Italian restaurant to share with me his recipe for one of the most delicious veal dishes I had ever tasted. Actually it was quite simple to prepare, and I soon discovered that sun-dried tomatoes provided the key to its unique taste.

In the original version of this dish, the chef used a generous amount of olive oil, which was excessively rich for my "reformed" taste and low-fat life style. Accordingly, when I tested the recipe for the revision, I substituted red wine for the oil. For those with an aversion to wine, try a little defatted chicken broth or tomato juice for the sauté process. However, I believe that the wine provides a touch of zest missing from even the original version. In any case, substituting a nonfat liquid for the oil in the recipe reduces the fat per serving by about 13 grams. Moreover, when chicken is substituted for veal, the fat content is reduced even further. Even the leanest veal available has about twice the saturated fat as chicken breast. I find little taste difference between the chicken and the veal in this recipe. In fact, knowing that I'm eliminating some extra fat and cholesterol with every bite, makes the chicken taste even better than the veal.

So, if you're in the mood for a chicken meal with an intense rich tomato flavor, try this one. It is a delight; and a spicy one, I assure you!

Traditional Recipe

2 cups water
3 ounces sun-dried tomatoes
¼ cup olive oil
4 cloves garlic, minced
4 scallions, finely chopped
1 pound thinly sliced veal cutlets
1 teaspoon dried basil
salt to taste
crushed red pepper to taste (optional)

Low-Fat Version

2 cups water
3 ounces sun-dried tomatoes
¼ cup red wine
4 cloves garlic, minced
4 scallions, finely chopped
1 pound thinly sliced chicken breast cutlets
1 teaspoon dried basil
sprinkle of salt
crushed red pepper to taste (optional)

Bring water to boil in small saucepan. Add sun-dried tomatoes and cook for 2 minutes. Drain tomatoes and reserve liquid. When cool, chop tomatoes and set aside. In a large skillet, sauté half of the garlic and all of the scallions in 2 tablespoons of oil until garlic is golden. Add tomatoes and half of the reserved liquid from the tomatoes. Blend thoroughly and simmer for about 5 minutes; then, remove tomato mixture from skillet. Heat remaining 2 tablespoons of oil in skillet; add remaining garlic and sauté until golden. Arrange veal cutlets in skillet, and season with basil and salt. Sauté until brown, turning occasionally. Spoon tomato mixture over veal. Add crushed red pepper, if desired, and simmer for about 15 minutes longer. Add a little more reserved tomato liquid to thin juices and prevent sticking, if necessary. (Serves 4)

PER SERVING

Calories:	329
Fat:	22.6 grams
Cholesterol:	84 milligrams

Bring water to boil in small saucepan. Add sun-dried tomatoes and cook for 2 minutes. Drain tomatoes and reserve liquid. When cool, chop tomatoes and set aside. In a large, nonstick skillet heat 2 tablespoons of the red wine. Add half of the garlic and all of the scallions and sauté for a minute or two. Add tomatoes and half of the reserved liquid from the tomatoes. Blend thoroughly and simmer for about 5 minutes; then, remove tomato mixture from skillet. Add remaining wine and remaining garlic to skillet and sauté for a minute. Arrange chicken cutlets in skillet, and season with basil and salt. Sauté until brown, turning occasionally. Spoon tomato mixture over chicken. Add crushed red pepper, if desired, and simmer for about 15 minutes longer. Add a little more reserved tomato liquid to thin juices and prevent sticking, if necessary. (Serves 4)

PER SERVING

Calories:	193
Fat:	4.4 grams
Cholesterol:	66 milligrams

Baked Turkey Cacciatore

For a slightly different tasting cacciatore dinner, try the low-fat version of Baked Turkey Cacciatore shown below. No doubt, you are familiar with the Italian classic, chicken cacciatore. One of the main differences between the two is that, while the original recipe starts with raw chicken, the Baked Turkey Cacciatore uses pre-cooked turkey—making it a terrific way to use the leftover bird from a holiday dinner. Naturally, leftover cooked chicken works well in this recipe, too, and may be substituted if you prefer chicken to turkey.

Compare the traditional and low-fat versions of this Italian variation. Notice that the use of oil, butter, and Parmesan cheese adds generous amounts of both fat and cholesterol to a seemingly heart-healthy turkey meal. In the low-fat revision, wine and Butter Buds replace the oil and butter used for sautéing. The Parmesan cheese is simply eliminated from the recipe, with minimal sacrifice in taste. I doubt that you'll feel deprived at all with the low-fat adaptation of this dish. It is a winner in both taste and nutrition!

Traditional Recipe

½ pound sliced mushrooms
2 tablespoons olive oil
2 tablespoons butter
2 medium onions, chopped
2 cloves garlic, minced
1 large green pepper,
    chopped into 1-inch
    pieces
1 tablespoon flour
2 cups crushed tomatoes
½ cup dry red wine
½ cup chicken broth
¼ teaspoon salt
½ teaspoon sugar
1 tablespoon parsley, minced
3 cups cooked turkey,
    chopped
½ cup Parmesan cheese

Low-Fat Version

½ pound sliced mushrooms
2 tablespoons white wine
    Butter Buds equivalent to
    2 tablespoons butter
2 medium onions, chopped
2 cloves garlic, minced
1 large green pepper,
    chopped into 1-inch
    pieces
1 tablespoon flour
2 cups crushed tomatoes
½ cup dry red wine
½ cup defatted chicken broth
¼ teaspoon salt
½ teaspoon sugar
3 cups cooked turkey,
    chopped
1 tablespoon parsley, minced

In a medium skillet, sauté mushrooms in 1 tablespoon of olive oil and 1 tablespoon of butter. In a large skillet, heat remaining oil and butter. Sauté onions and garlic until tender. Add green pepper and cook for 3 more minutes. Sprinkle flour over vegetables and stir until blended. Add tomatoes, wine, broth, salt, and sugar. Reduce heat and simmer about 20 minutes, uncovered. Add mushrooms and parsley, and cook 10 minutes longer. Spoon about half of the sauce into an oblong baking dish. Arrange turkey over sauce and top with remaining sauce. Cover with foil and bake at 350° for 30 minutes. Uncover and bake for 15 minutes longer. Sprinkle with Parmesan cheese during the last 5 minutes of baking. (Serves 4)

PER SERVING

Calories:	382
Fat:	19 grams
Cholesterol:	78 milligrams

In a medium, nonstick skillet, sauté mushrooms in a mixture of half the white wine and half the Butter Buds. In a large skillet, heat remaining wine and Butter Buds. Sauté onions and garlic until tender. Add green pepper and cook for 3 more minutes. Sprinkle flour over vegetables and stir until blended. Add tomatoes, wine, broth, salt, and sugar. Reduce heat and simmer about 20 minutes, uncovered. Add mushrooms and cook 10 minutes longer. Spoon about half of the sauce into an oblong baking dish. Arrange turkey over sauce and top with remaining sauce. Cover with foil and bake at 350° for 30 minutes. Sprinkle with minced parsley and bake, uncovered, for 15 minutes longer. (Serves 4)

PER SERVING

Calories:	231
Fat:	2.9 grams
Cholesterol:	52 milligrams

Pineapple-Glazed Ham

There was a time when a baked ham dinner wasn't even considered to be a meal choice for those concerned about the amount of fat and cholesterol in their diets. Now, with a little care in selection, a ham lover can once again enjoy an occasional lean turkey ham dinner. The operative words are: occasional, lean, and turkey! As with all cured, smoked, or processed meats, consumption should be limited. Although we have available to us a vast array of processed poultry products such as sausage, bologna, kielbasa, and frankfurters, many are not much lower in fat than similar products made with beef and pork. Most contain large amounts of sodium and significantly higher amounts of fat than plain chicken or turkey. So, when you select a ham, or any of these products, read the label carefully. Make certain that the product does not derive more than 30 percent of its calories from fat. For example, it should not exceed 3 grams of fat for every 100 calorie portion. Actually, the 20 percent rule, or 2 grams of fat for every 100 calories is preferable, but it is hard to come by when selecting turkey ham. Also, if you are on a very strict low sodium diet, this may be one meal that you'll want to pass by, or consume very sparingly and only on rare occasions.

Finally, never buy a turkey ham without a label containing nutrient values. The absence of such information may mean that it's not much of a bargain, nutritionally speaking. Remember, not all turkey hams are created equal!

Traditional Recipe

1 small, lean boneless ham
   (about 2 pounds)
½ cup brown sugar
1 cup unsweetened crushed
   pineapple in juice
   (drain and reserve juice)
2 teaspoons mustard
¼ teaspoon ground cloves

Pineapple-Glazed Turkey Ham Low-Fat Version

1 small, lean turkey ham
   (about 2 pounds)
½ cup brown sugar
1 cup unsweetened crushed
   pineapple in juice
   (drain and reserve juice)
2 teaspoons mustard
¼ teaspoon ground cloves

Place ham in small shallow roasting pan and set aside. In a small saucepan, combine brown sugar and juice from crushed pineapple. Heat until sugar is dissolved. Add mustard, ground cloves, and crushed pineapple. Blend thoroughly and continue heating until mixture bubbles. Pour over ham. Bake uncovered at 350° for 1 hour. Add a small amount of water if juice evaporates while baking. Slice ham, arrange on platter, and spoon on crushed pineapple and juices that remain in pan. (Serves 8)

Per Serving

Calories: 252
Fat: 9.4 grams
Cholesterol: 88 milligrams

Place turkey ham in small, shallow roasting pan and set aside. In a small saucepan, combine brown sugar and juice from crushed pineapple. Heat until sugar is dissolved. Add mustard, ground cloves, and crushed pineapple. Blend thoroughly and continue heating until mixture bubbles. Pour over turkey ham. Bake uncovered at 350° for 1 hour. Add a small amount of water if juice evaporates while baking. Slice ham, arrange on platter, and spoon on crushed pineapple and juices that remain in pan. (Serves 8)

Per Serving

Calories: 202
Fat: 5.1 grams
Cholesterol: 62 milligrams

Breaded Veal Cutlets

Veal cutlet is about as important to an Italian meal plan as is pasta. It offers a great deal of versatility in preparation, which is one reason it is a favorite in many Italian recipes.

When I was a child, one of the typical veal dishes that appeared on the dinner table regularly was breaded and fried veal cutlet. Because it tasted equally good hot or cold, a sandwich of breaded veal cutlet on fresh Italian bread was a favorite food item for summer picnics.

At that time, no one cared much about saturated fat, cholesterol, or total dietary fat. Years later people realized that chicken cutlets were a good substitute for veal. However, it was not the lower saturated fat content of chicken that motivated the switch from veal to chicken, but rather the fact that the price of veal was becoming exorbitant. Even when chicken replaced veal, the method of preparation remained unchanged. Frying in olive oil was still the method of choice for most people. Except for ardent dieters, no one paid much attention to the excessive amount of fat used to fry the cutlets. Even when cholesterol consciousness first became fashionable, I always felt that as long as I was frying in cholesterol-free olive oil, I need not be concerned. It was much later when I learned that a heart-healthy diet meant reducing total fat, not just saturated fat and cholesterol. This meant cutting back on the added fat used in food preparation. Armed with this new information, I began making my cutlets by breading and baking, instead of frying. The results are noteworthy.

Compare the calories, fat, and cholesterol content of the two cutlet recipes below. The higher fat and calorie count in the recipe is due primarily to the use of oil for frying; while the yolk of the egg is responsible for the significant amount of cholesterol per serving. Remember also, the quantity of fat in each serving of veal cutlet is a conservative number because, in most cases, more than ½ cup of oil is required to fry a pound of breaded cutlet. So, try the Breaded Chicken Cutlets recipe. You'll save money by eliminating oil. You won't have to deal with the messy cleanup of a greasy stove and skillet. And, you'll do your heart a big favor as well!

Traditional Recipe

1 pound veal cutlets, thinly sliced
2 eggs, beaten
1 cup seasoned bread crumbs
½ cup olive oil

Breaded Chicken Cutlets Low-Fat Version

1 cup cornflake crumbs
1 teaspoon Italian herb seasoning
1 pound chicken cutlets, thinly sliced
2 egg whites, beaten
1 lemon, cut into wedges

Dip veal cutlets into egg; then press into crumbs, coating well on both sides. Heat oil in large skillet. Sauté cutlets in hot oil until golden brown on both sides. Remove cutlets from skillet and place on paper towel to drain excess oil. (Serves 4)

Per Serving

Calories:	535
Fat:	35.9 grams
Cholesterol:	190 milligrams

Combine cornflake crumbs and Italian herb seasoning. Dip chicken cutlets into egg whites; then press into seasoned cornflake crumbs. Place cutlets on nonstick cookie sheet and bake at 375° for 10 minutes on each side. (Do not over bake. Thinner cutlets may require less baking time.) When cooked, remove cutlets to serving platter and squeeze on lemon juice. (Serves 4)

Per Serving

Calories:	275
Fat:	4.2 grams
Cholesterol:	66 milligrams

🍒 *Stuffed Boneless Chicken Breasts*

One of the problems I struggled with after embarking on a low-fat life style was the issue of cooking for dinner guests. Should I cook differently for them? Of course not! To do so would be to concede that low-fat foods are inferior in taste and are not of suitable quality for dinner guests. While that may be true for some low-fat meals, I vowed it would not apply to meals from my kitchen! If a meal did not taste good enough to serve to others, it would not be served to my family.

I suggest you try the following recipe for your next dinner party. Unless your guests have an aversion to chicken, the low-fat recipe for Stuffed Boneless Chicken Breasts will surely wow them! It offers ease of preparation coupled with a gourmet quality that will convince them that you spent hours in the kitchen preparing their dinner.

When you compare the calories, fat, and cholesterol content of both versions of the recipe, you will discover the effects of added fats, such as butter and oil. The original recipe contains double the calories and cholesterol and over ten times the fat as the revised recipe.

Traditional Recipe

- ½ cup water
- 6 tablespoons butter
- ½ cup chopped onions
- 1½ cups herb-seasoned stuffing mix
- ¼ teaspoon garlic powder black pepper to taste, if desired
- ¼ cup raisins
- ¼ cup finely chopped water chestnuts
- 4 boneless chicken breast halves, skinned
- 2 tablespoons olive oil
- ¼ cup rose wine
- 2 tablespoons melted butter

Low-Fat Version

- ½ cup water Butter Buds equivalent to 6 tablespoons butter
- ½ cup chopped onions
- 4 slices nonfat wheat bread, toasted and cubed (or pita bread)
- ½ teaspoon oregano
- ¼ teaspoon garlic powder salt and pepper to taste
- ¼ cup raisins
- ¼ cup finely chopped water chestnuts
- 4 boneless chicken breast halves, skinned
- ¼ cup rose wine Butter Buds equivalent to 2 tablespoons butter
- ½ teaspoon cornstarch (optional)

In a medium saucepan, boil water. Add 6 tablespoons butter and onions. Simmer for about 3 to 4 minutes. Remove from heat. Add stuffing mix and toss until water is absorbed. Season with garlic powder and black pepper, if desired. Fold in raisins and water chestnuts.

Lay chicken breast halves on flat surface and pound with a meat mallet to ¼-inch thickness. Arrange a quarter of the stuffing in the center of each chicken breast half. Fold in the sides and roll up. Fasten with toothpicks or wrap with clean white string.

In a large skillet, heat olive oil. Add chicken breasts and sauté until brown on all sides. Combine wine and melted butter, and add to skillet. Cover and simmer for about 40 minutes, or until chicken is tender, turning occasionally. If necessary, add a small amount of water to prevent sticking. (Serves 4)

PER SERVING

Calories:	540
Fat:	35.1 grams
Cholesterol:	145 milligrams

In a medium saucepan, boil water. Add Butter Buds (equal to 6 tablespoons butter) and onions. Simmer for about 3 to 4 minutes. Remove from heat. Add bread cubes and toss until water is absorbed. Season with oregano, garlic powder, salt, and pepper. Fold in raisins and water chestnuts.

Lay chicken breast halves on flat surface and pound with a meat mallet to ¼-inch thickness. Arrange a quarter of the stuffing in the center of each chicken breast half. Fold in the sides and roll up. Fasten with toothpicks or wrap with clean white string.

In a nonstick skillet, sauté chicken breasts in a tablespoon of wine for about 5 minutes, turning to brown on all sides. Combine remaining wine and Butter Buds, and add to skillet. Cover and simmer for about 40 minutes, or until chicken is tender, turning occasionally. If necessary, add water to prevent sticking. Thicken pan juices with cornstarch during last minute of cooking time, if desired. (Serves 4)

PER SERVING

Calories:	245
Fat:	3.3 grams
Cholesterol:	73 milligrams

Ham Steak Veronique

Some things just naturally go together —strawberries and cream, Bogey and Bacall, Halloween and pumpkins, movies and popcorn. Likewise, it seemed to me that ham and pineapple were a natural pair. Then a TV chef introduced me to an interesting alternative to the pineapple. It is an apple-grape sauce made with chopped apples and white seedless grapes.

Prepared according to the original Ham Steak Veronique recipe, ordinary ham steak is sautéed in butter until brown. Then the apple-grape sauce is prepared and combined with the ham steak.

The revised Ham Steak Veronique recipe retains most of the flavor of the original recipe. Naturally, I had to make some changes to comply with my established low-fat criteria. I replaced ordinary ham with lean turkey ham to reduce saturated fat. In addition, I eliminated the olive oil and butter and used appropriate substitutes in their place. Butter Buds provides the buttery flavor without the calories and fat of ordinary butter. Also, I used defatted chicken broth instead of ordinary beef or chicken stock, with no noticeable change in taste. It is amazing how many calories and grams of fat one can eliminate by simply refrigerating the chicken broth and skimming off the layer of fat that congeals on the surface.

Converting this recipe from the traditional to the low-fat version required little effort and the benefits, as seen in the nutrient values, are well worth it, especially for those monitoring their intake of calories, fat, and cholesterol. Equally appealing is the fact that the low-fat version offers such great taste.

Traditional Recipe

1 tablespoon olive oil
1 medium apple (peeled, cored, and chopped)
1 medium onion, chopped
2 tablespoons apple juice
1 tablespoon cornstarch
½ cup chicken or beef stock
20 seedless white grapes, cut in halves
2 tablespoons butter
4 small ham steaks (about 4 ounces each)

Low-Fat Version

2 tablespoons apple juice
1 medium apple (peeled, cored, and chopped)
1 medium onion, chopped
1 tablespoon cornstarch
½ cup defatted chicken broth
20 seedless white grapes, cut in halves
1 pound lean turkey ham, cut into 4 "ham steak" slices
Butter Buds equivalent to 2 tablespoons butter
2 tablespoons white wine

In a medium skillet, sauté apple and onion in olive oil until onion is translucent. Add apple juice and continue cooking. Dissolve cornstarch in stock and add to skillet, blending thoroughly. Continue heating until juices thicken. Add grapes and toss. Set aside. In a large skillet, sauté the ham steaks in butter until brown on both sides. Spoon grape sauce over steaks and heat thoroughly before serving. (Serves 4)

Per Serving

Calories: 351
Fat: 20 grams
Cholesterol: 118 milligrams

In a medium nonstick skillet, heat apple juice. Add chopped apple and onion, and sauté until onion is translucent. Dissolve cornstarch in chicken broth and add to skillet, blending thoroughly. Continue heating until juices thicken. Add grapes and toss. Set aside. Pan-fry the turkey ham steaks in a large, dry, nonstick skillet over medium-high heat. After the steaks are seared on both sides, combine the Butter Buds and wine and add to the skillet. Turn the steaks to coat on both sides with the wine mixture. Spoon the grape sauce over the steaks and heat thoroughly before serving. (Serves 4)

Per Serving

Calories: 225
Fat: 4.3 grams
Cholesterol: 80 milligrams

Stuffed Beef Bracciola

The recipe for Stuffed Beef Bracciola was not removed from my recipe file when I made the decision to eliminate red meat from my diet. Instead, I simply substituted turkey breast cutlets for the round steak, which reduced the saturated fat. Although round steak is one of the leanest cuts of beef, it still contains about four times the saturated fat as turkey breast.

In addition to substituting turkey for beef, two other changes were made in the original recipe. Butter was replaced with Butter Buds and red wine was used instead of olive oil to sauté the bracciola. Approximately 220 calories and 25 grams of fat were removed from each serving by removing the butter and oil from the recipe. Even if you use the round steak instead of the turkey breast, it makes sense to eliminate the butter and oil. Both are 99 percent fat, and our goal should be to reduce not just saturated fats, but all fats in our diet. Cutting back on the added fats used in the cooking process brings us a step closer to that goal.

Clearly, there is no contest between the traditional and low-fat version of bracciola with regard to nutrient values. The Turkey Bracciola is definitely the heart-healthy winner!

Traditional Recipe

½ cup water
6 tablespoons butter
½ cup chopped onions
4 slices white bread toasted and cubed
½ teaspoon oregano
¼ teaspoon garlic powder
½ teaspoon salt (or to taste)
  pepper to taste
¼ cup raisins
4 thinly sliced round steak cutlets (about 1 pound)
2 tablespoons olive oil
1 28-ounce can crushed tomatoes in purée
1 tablespoon minced fresh parsley

Stuffed Turkey Bracciola Low-Fat Version

½ cup water
  Butter Buds equivalent to 6 tablespoons butter (diluted in about ¼ cup warm water)
½ cup chopped onions
4 slices nonfat wheat bread, toasted and cubed
½ teaspoon oregano
¼ teaspoon garlic powder
½ teaspoon salt (or to taste)
  pepper to taste
¼ cup raisins
1 pound turkey breast cutlets, thinly sliced
2 tablespoons red wine
1 28-ounce can crushed tomatoes in purée
1 tablespoon minced fresh parsley

Boil water. Add butter and onions. Simmer for 5 minutes. Add bread cubes and toss until water is absorbed. Add more water, if necessary. Season with oregano, garlic powder, salt, and pepper. Fold in raisins. Arrange cutlets on a flat surface and place a quarter of the stuffing in the center of each cutlet. Roll cutlet around stuffing in jelly-roll fashion and fasten with a toothpick. Sauté beef rolls in olive oil, gently turning to brown on all sides. Add tomatoes, cover, and simmer for 1 hour, or until tender. Sprinkle with minced parsley before serving. (Serves 4)

PER SERVING

Calories:	526
Fat:	36.1 grams
Cholesterol:	132 milligrams

Boil water. Add Butter Buds and onions. Simmer for 5 minutes. Add bread cubes and toss until water is absorbed. For a moister stuffing, add more water. Season with oregano, garlic powder, salt, and pepper. Fold in raisins. Arrange cutlets on a flat surface and place a quarter of the stuffing in the center of each cutlet. Roll cutlet around stuffing in jelly-roll fashion and fasten with a toothpick. Sauté turkey rolls in wine in large, nonstick skillet for 5 minutes, gently turning to coat with wine on all sides. Add tomatoes, cover, and simmer for 1 hour, or until tender. Sprinkle with minced parsley before serving. (Serves 4)

PER SERVING

Calories:	278
Fat:	2.5 grams
Cholesterol:	66 milligrams

Hawaiian Chicken

In general, poultry is considered to be lower in fat than red meat. However, this may not always be the case. For example, depending on the cut, beef may contain anywhere from 33 percent to 83 percent fat. Interestingly, some types of poultry, such as goose, duck, and pheasant, contain as much as 77 percent fat. Chicken and turkey, on the other hand, usually range between 12 percent and 30 percent fat. Remember, the white meat of each contains less fat than the dark meat. Of course, these estimates for chicken and turkey are contingent upon removal of the skin and underlying fat. If the skin and underlying fat are not removed the fat content of the chicken or turkey triples, thereby minimizing the effectiveness of each as low-fat sources of animal protein. Do not forget to remove the skin and trim all visible fat from your poultry before cooking. Then, use the meat as your replacement for red meat in some of your favorite recipes.

Look at the two versions of Hawaiian Chicken that follow. In the traditional recipe no reference is made to removing the skin. In addition, butter, a known offender to a low-fat, low-cholesterol diet, is listed as an ingredient. Obviously, both the chicken skin and the butter had to be eliminated in the revised recipe. These changes were the only ones required to convert this recipe to an acceptable low-fat, low-cholesterol entrée.

Even if you decide not to try this recipe, make a note of the grams of fat in each version—and remember these numbers the next time you reach for a piece of chicken with skin!

Traditional Recipe

4 chicken breast quarters
½ cup green pepper strips
½ cup red pepper strips
4 tablespoons butter, melted
8 ounces crushed pineapple in juice
2 tablespoons prepared mustard
2 tablespoons honey
1 teaspoon rum-flavored extract

Low-Fat Version

4 boneless chicken breasts (no skin)
½ cup green pepper strips
½ cup red pepper strips
Butter Buds equivalent to 4 tablespoons butter
8 ounces crushed pineapple in juice
2 tablespoons prepared mustard
2 tablespoons honey
1 teaspoon rum-flavored extract

Arrange chicken in a lightly-greased, shallow baking pan. Distribute pepper strips evenly over chicken. In a small bowl, combine butter, crushed pineapple in juice, mustard, honey, and rum extract. Spoon over chicken. Bake uncovered in a 400° oven for 1 hour. If necessary, add a small amount of water to prevent sticking. (Serves 4)

PER SERVING

Calories:	389
Fat:	25.3 grams
Cholesterol:	111 milligrams

Arrange chicken in shallow, nonstick baking pan. Distribute pepper strips evenly over chicken. In a small bowl, combine Butter Buds, crushed pineapple in juice, mustard, honey, and rum extract. Spoon over chicken. Bake uncovered in a 400° oven for 1 hour. If necessary, add a small amount of water to prevent sticking. (Serves 4)

PER SERVING

Calories:	230
Fat:	4.6 grams
Cholesterol:	66 milligrams

Eliminating red meat from my diet was not a hardship for me—with one exception. Lamb had always been my favorite red meat, and I thoroughly enjoyed all cuts. In fact, I even preferred ground lamb to ground beef for burgers.

Recently, I spooned some mint jelly over a ground turkey patty I was eating. It reminded me of lamb with mint jelly. In fact, for a moment, I actually thought I was eating lamb. It occurred to me that I might resurrect an old favorite ground lamb recipe and convert it to a low-fat version by substituting ground turkey for the lamb, along with other appropriate changes. A glance at the recipe revealed that the only other changes necessary were the replacement of the whole egg with egg whites, or egg substitute, and the use of nonfat bread, instead of regular bread crumbs. These changes resulted in a reduction per serving of 20 grams of fat and 40 milligrams of cholesterol.

Ironically, when I eat these turkey patties sprinkled with lemon juice and coated with mint jelly, I am transported back to the days when lamb was a regular part of my diet. Obviously, I am not suggesting that ground turkey tastes like lamb. However, when a turkey patty is coated with mint jelly, it is the jelly that provides the dominant taste. It is hard to tell that the jelly is covering turkey, not lamb!

Traditional Recipe

1 pound ground lamb
1 egg
½ cup soft bread crumbs
¼ cup chopped ripe olives
¼ cup chopped fresh parsley
2 cloves garlic, minced
¼ teaspoon cinnamon
⅛ teaspoon nutmeg
   salt and pepper to taste
1 lemon, cut into 4 wedges
2 teaspoons mint jelly
   freshly ground black
      pepper

Ground Turkey Patties with Mint Jelly
Low-Fat Version

1 pound ground turkey meat
   (no skin)
   egg substitute equivalent to
      1 egg
½ cup soft bread crumbs from
      nonfat "lite" bread
¼ cup chopped ripe olives
¼ cup chopped fresh parsley
2 cloves garlic, minced
¼ teaspoon cinnamon
⅛ teaspoon nutmeg
   salt and pepper (optional)
1 lemon, cut into 4 wedges
2 teaspoons mint jelly
   freshly ground black
      pepper

In a large bowl, combine all ingredients and mix well. Divide mixture evenly into 4 portions, and shape into ½-inch-thick oval patties. Broil about 4 inches from heat for about 5 minutes on each side, or to desired degree of doneness. Serve with a squeeze of lemon juice. Top with a spread of mint jelly and freshly ground black pepper. (Serves 4)

PER SERVING

Calories:	362
Fat:	25 grams
Cholesterol:	125 milligrams

In a large bowl, combine all ingredients and mix well. Divide mixture evenly into 4 portions, and shape into ½-inch-thick oval patties. Broil about 4 inches from heat for about 5 minutes on each side, or until turkey meat is no longer pink in color. Serve with a squeeze of lemon juice. Top with a spread of mint jelly and freshly ground black pepper. (Serves 4)

PER SERVING

Calories:	220
Fat:	5.1 grams
Cholesterol:	84 milligrams

🍒 Veal and Mushrooms with Vermicelli

The following veal and mushrooms recipe offers a variety of meal options. It can be served with or without spaghetti, as a main course, as a side dish, over cooked rice, or even chilled and stuffed into a pita pocket for lunch!

My introduction to this tasty wine-flavored treat took place in a gourmet Italian restaurant known for its fixed menu, which consists of an eight-course Italian feast. In this restaurant, the recipe was prepared as an entrée and served in a small casserole, as one would serve tenderloin tips.

The restaurant menu listed a brief description of the main ingredients and method of preparation for each course. The caption for this meal read, "tender veal tips gently sautéed with mushrooms and black olives in a butter-wine sauce." The restaurant also provided guests with complimentary recipe cards for each selection from the eight-course meal. Aided by my handy calculator, it took only minutes to get the scoop on the quantity of hidden fat in this savory fare. The use of butter and oil added about 50 grams of fat to the recipe, which naturally resulted in higher calories, as well.

In the revised version, all added fats for sautéing are eliminated, and the use of Butter Buds with white wine provides the butter-wine flavor. To further reduce fat, boneless chicken breast cutlets replace veal.

Serving the finished product over vermicelli is a personal preference. However, served in any of the suggested ways, this dish is appealing and delicious. Even more important, the converted recipe is a healthy one as well!

Traditional Recipe

2 tablespoons olive oil
2 cloves garlic, minced
¾ pound veal cutlets, cut into bite-size strips
¼ cup white wine
4 tablespoons butter
2 small cans sliced mushrooms, drained
10 ripe olives, chopped
1 tablespoon chopped fresh parsley
1 tablespoon chopped fresh basil
salt and pepper to taste
¼ teaspoon crushed red pepper (optional)
1 pound vermicelli, cooked

Chicken and Mushrooms with Vermicelli Low-Fat Version

½ cup white wine
2 cloves garlic, minced
¾ pound chicken breast cutlets, sliced into bite-size strips
Butter Buds equivalent to 8 tablespoons butter
2 small cans sliced mushrooms, drained
10 ripe olives, chopped
1 tablespoon chopped fresh parsley
1 tablespoon chopped fresh basil
salt and pepper to taste
¼ teaspoon crushed red pepper (optional)
1 pound vermicelli, cooked

In a large skillet, sauté garlic in oil until golden. Add veal and continue to sauté for about 5 minutes. Add wine, butter, mushrooms, olives, parsley, basil, salt, pepper, and red pepper, if desired. Blend ingredients and continue sautéing over medium heat for about 10 minutes, stirring frequently. Spoon over cooked vermicelli. (Serves 6)

PER SERVING

Calories:	471
Fat:	22.9 grams
Cholesterol:	82 milligrams

In a large, nonstick skillet, heat 2 tablespoons wine. Add minced garlic and chicken strips and sauté for about 5 minutes, stirring constantly. Add remaining wine, Butter Buds, mushrooms, olives, parsley, basil, salt, pepper, and red pepper, if desired. Blend ingredients and continue sautéing over medium heat for about 10 minutes, stirring frequently. Spoon over cooked vermicelli. (Serves 6)

PER SERVING

Calories:	343
Fat:	4.7 grams
Cholesterol:	44 milligrams

🍒 Sweet and Sour Chicken

The traditional version of this Sweet and Sour Chicken dish needed very little modification to convert it to a heart-healthy fare. Moreover, the changes made did not detract from its delightful Polynesian flavor.

In the original recipe, assorted chicken parts are first pan-fried in oil and then transferred to a cookie sheet, glazed with sweet and sour sauce, and baked to perfection. However, in order to retain the moistness of the skinless chicken breast in the revised recipe, the entire cooking process takes place in the skillet, rather than in the oven. Skinless chicken tends to become dry when baked for longer than 15 minutes. Of course, removal of the skin has its clear-cut advantages, as is evident when one compares the nutrient values—especially fat content—listed with each recipe.

Note too that cornstarch is eliminated from the revised recipe because the natural evaporation process that occurs while cooking in the skillet causes the sauce to thicken without the need for a thickening agent.

Another modification that resulted in reduced fat content of the converted recipe was the substitution of white wine for the peanut oil used to fry the chicken. Naturally, defatted chicken broth, or any nonfat liquid, may be used instead of oil if wine is not available.

A piece of chicken skin and a tablespoon or two of oil may go unnoticed, or may even seem harmless, to those with an untrained eye for reducing fat and cholesterol in the diet. Some people are aware of the fat present in chicken skin and might remove the skin while dining. However, in a recipe such as this, if the skin is discarded after cooking, you lose most of the flavor of the glaze along with it. So begin with skinless chicken. The result will be, not only a healthier meal, but a tastier one, as well!

Traditional Recipe

- 2 tablespoons peanut oil
- 1 pound chicken parts
- ¼ teaspoon garlic powder
  salt and pepper to taste
- ¼ cup vinegar (any variety)
- ¼ cup sugar
- 2 tablespoons orange juice
- 2 tablespoons pineapple juice
- 2 tablespoons tomato paste
- 1 tablespoon cornstarch

Low-Fat Version

- 4 boneless chicken breast halves
- 2 tablespoons white wine
- ¼ teaspoon garlic powder
  salt and pepper to taste
- ¼ cup vinegar (any variety)
- ¼ cup sugar
- 2 tablespoons orange juice
- 2 tablespoons pineapple juice
- 2 tablespoons tomato paste

In a large skillet, heat oil. Add chicken parts, garlic powder, salt, and pepper, and sauté until brown on all sides. In a small saucepan, combine vinegar, sugar, orange juice, pineapple juice, and tomato paste, blending thoroughly. Add cornstarch and heat until thick and bubbly. Arrange chicken parts on a cookie sheet. With a pastry brush, coat chicken evenly on all sides with sauce. Bake at 400° for about 30 minutes. (Baking time will vary with size of chicken parts.) (Serves 4)

PER SERVING

Calories:	355
Fat:	18.4 grams
Cholesterol:	66 milligrams

Place chicken in a large, nonstick skillet with wine. Season on both sides with garlic powder, salt, and pepper. Sauté for about 5 minutes on each side. Combine vinegar, sugar, orange juice, pineapple juice, and tomato paste. Blend thoroughly. Spoon sauce over chicken, coating evenly on all sides. Cover and simmer for about 30 minutes, or until chicken is tender. (Serves 4)

PER SERVING

Calories:	242
Fat:	4.5 grams
Cholesterol:	66 milligrams

🐛 Chicken with Preserves

If you have a sweet tooth, you will adore this recipe for Chicken with Preserves. In fact, I find it easy to skip dessert when I've eaten this meal, because it diminishes my usual desire for a sweet treat following dinner. Consider the calories saved by skipping dessert! However, even with a modest dessert, the low-fat version of this recipe is a terrific choice for health-conscious, calorie-counting individuals. To reduce calories even more, a low-calorie fruit spread may be used in place of the usual type. Although the following recipes call for pineapple preserves, other flavors work equally well. Use your favorite.

When you compare the nutrient values at the end of each recipe, you will notice that the traditional version has five times the amount of fat per serving than the low-fat version. This excess is due to the use of oil and butter. In the revised recipe, the oil and butter have been replaced with wine and Butter Buds, resulting in a healthier chicken dinner.

In addition to its nutritional soundness, this recipe can be varied. For example, use fruit juice in place of wine. Try to coordinate the variety of juice with the flavor of preserves or fruit spread. That is, use pineapple juice with pineapple preserves, orange juice with orange marmalade, apple juice with apple jelly, and so on. Put on your creative thinking cap and dispel the myth that chicken is chicken. It can be anything you want it to be. Use mint jelly and think lamb, or use apple jelly and think pork. I do!

Traditional Recipe

2 tablespoons olive oil
1 clove garlic, minced
1 pound boneless chicken
    breast (about 4 breast
    halves)
¼ teaspoon oregano
¼ teaspoon dried sweet basil
3 tablespoons all fruit
    pineapple spread or
    preserves
2 tablespoons butter
2 tablespoons water

Low-Fat Version

2 tablespoons white wine
1 clove garlic, minced
1 pound boneless chicken
    breast (about 4 halves)
¼ teaspoon oregano
¼ teaspoon dried sweet basil
3 tablespoons all fruit
    pineapple spread or
    preserves
    Butter Buds equivalent to 4
    tablespoons butter
¼ cup water

In a large skillet, sauté garlic in oil until golden. Add chicken, oregano, and basil and cook for about 10 minutes until brown on all sides. Meanwhile, place fruit preserves, butter, and water in small saucepan and heat for a minute or two until ingredients are well-blended. Spoon fruit sauce over chicken, turning chicken to coat on all sides. Cover skillet and simmer chicken for 30 minutes, turning occasionally. Add a little water, if necessary, to thin sauce and prevent sticking. (Serves 4)

Per Serving

Calories:	342
Fat:	15.9 grams
Cholesterol:	84 milligrams

In a large, nonstick skillet, sauté chicken, garlic, oregano, and basil in white wine for about 10 minutes, turning to brown on all sides. Add a little water if wine evaporates while cooking. Meanwhile, place fruit preserves, Butter Buds, and water in small saucepan and heat for a minute or two until ingredients are well-blended. Spoon fruit sauce over chicken, turning chicken to coat on all sides. Cover skillet and simmer chicken for 30 minutes, turning occasionally. Add a little water, if necessary to thin sauce and prevent sticking. (Serves 4)

Per Serving

Calories:	240
Fat:	3.1 grams
Cholesterol:	66 milligrams

🍒 *Honey-Mustard Glazed Chicken*

If you are like most health-conscious Americans, you are undoubtedly eating more chicken and fish these days. Be mindful, however, to go the extra mile and remove the skin from your chicken, or you may be offsetting any good you are attempting to accomplish.

Two versions of an easy-to-prepare chicken dish follow. In the traditional version of the recipe, the chicken breasts are baked with the skin and glazed with a mixture of melted butter, lemon juice, honey, and mustard. In the revised, low-fat version, the chicken skin is removed and the chicken is cooked partially in boiling water before baking. When baking skinless chicken, it is always a good idea to parboil it first. This reduces the baking time and allows the chicken to retain moistness. Another change made in the revised version is the replacement of butter with Butter Buds, which provides buttery taste without the added fat and cholesterol.

For people on the go, the low-fat version is a wonderful fast meal to prepare. The chicken can be boiled ahead of time and refrigerated. Then it can be glazed and popped into the oven for 20 minutes for an easy chicken dinner. A glance at the nutrient values illustrates the merits of the low-fat version as well!

Traditional Recipe

2 large chicken breasts (4 halves)
2 tablespoons melted butter
2 tablespoons lemon juice
1/4 cup honey
2 tablespoons mustard

Low-Fat Version

2 large skinless chicken breasts (4 halves)
Butter Buds equivalent to 2 tablespoons butter
2 tablespoons lemon juice
1/4 cup honey
2 tablespoons mustard

Place chicken parts in shallow baking pan, skin side up. Combine melted butter, lemon juice, honey, and mustard. Blend well. Using a pastry brush, spread glaze over chicken. Place chicken into 350° oven and bake uncovered for about 45–60 minutes, or until done. Turn chicken and brush occasionally with additional glaze while baking. (Serves 4)

PER SERVING

Calories: 319
Fat: 14.4 grams
Cholesterol: 101 milligrams

Place chicken parts in soup pot. Cover with water and bring to a boil. Reduce heat and parboil for 15 minutes. Remove chicken from water and place in shallow baking pan. Dissolve Butter Buds in lemon juice. Add honey and mustard and blend well. Using a pastry brush, spread glaze over chicken parts. Place chicken into 350° oven and bake uncovered for about 20 minutes, turning and brushing occasionally with additional glaze. (Serves 4)

PER SERVING

Calories: 217
Fat: 3.4 grams
Cholesterol: 73 milligrams

🍒 *Monte Cristo Sandwich*

Add a cup of soup and a tossed salad to a Monte Cristo Sandwich and you have a wonderful meal, any day of the week. It makes a great change of pace for an evening meal and is a delicious choice for Sunday brunch when served with maple syrup.

Note the changes necessary to bring the original recipe into compliance with a low-fat, low-cholesterol life style. In the original recipe, a sandwich made with ham, cheese, and turkey on white bread is dipped into beaten egg and toasted on a griddle with ample amounts of butter. In the revised version turkey ham replaces the regular ham, and the cheese is replaced with tomato slices. Since I eliminated the cheese, I added tomatoes to add moisture to the sandwich that would have been provided by the melted cheese. The sandwich is made with whole wheat "lite" bread, which generally contains no shortening and has less than 1 gram of fat per slice. It is then dipped into a mixture of egg substitute and Butter Buds and grilled on a nonstick griddle. Serve plain, with a sprinkle of powdered sugar, or with a drizzle of maple syrup.

Now let's tally the savings in calories, fat, and cholesterol. The traditional version contains 570 calories more than the revised version! In addition, the elimination of butter, cheese, and eggs saves over 50 grams of fat and 350 milligrams of cholesterol. Moreover, the switch to turkey ham helps cut back on the amount of saturated fat in the sandwich. The benefit associated with replacing the whole egg with egg substitute is common knowledge for those on low-cholesterol diets. This step alone eliminates a hefty 213 milligrams of cholesterol. The switch to "lite" wheat bread further reduces calories and adds fiber, as well.

Without hesitation, I highly recommend switching your method of preparing Monte Cristo Sandwiches to the low-fat recipe shown below. It is a great way to enjoy an old favorite, without abandoning your diet.

Traditional Recipe

2 slices white bread
1 ounce sliced ham
1 ounce sliced turkey
1 ounce sliced American cheese
1 egg, beaten
3 tablespoons butter
powdered sugar and maple syrup to taste

Low-Fat Version

2 slices whole wheat "lite" bread
1 ounce sliced lean turkey ham
1 ounce sliced chicken breast or turkey breast
2 slices tomato
salt and pepper to taste (optional)
Butter Buds equivalent to 2 tablespoons butter
egg substitute equal to 1 egg
sprinkle of powdered sugar (optional)
1 tablespoon maple syrup (optional)

Arrange ham, turkey, and cheese on one slice of buttered bread. Top with second slice of buttered bread. Dip sandwich into beaten egg, coating evenly on both sides. Melt remaining butter on griddle over medium heat. Grill sandwich on both sides until golden brown. Serve warm with a sprinkle of powdered sugar and maple syrup, if desired. (Serves 1)

Per Serving

Calories:	795
Fat:	62.4 grams
Cholesterol:	395 milligrams

Arrange turkey ham, chicken breast, and tomato slices on one slice of bread. Season to taste with salt and pepper, if desired. Top with second slice of bread. Combine egg substitute and dry Butter Buds and blend until dissolved. Dip sandwich into mixture, coating evenly on both sides. Grill on nonstick skillet over medium heat until golden brown on both sides. Serve warm with a sprinkle of powdered sugar and maple syrup, if desired. (Serves 1)

Per Serving

Calories:	228
Fat:	2.2 grams
Cholesterol:	50 milligrams

Stuffed Flounder

For people watching their fat and cholesterol intake Stuffed Flounder seems to be a wise, heart-healthy selection. The two versions of Stuffed Flounder that follow are identical, with the exception of one ingredient. The traditional version uses butter and the revised version uses Butter Buds. For years I prepared my Stuffed Flounder according to the traditional recipe. However, knowing that butter was loaded with saturated fat (the worst kind), I substituted polyunsaturated margarine to ease my conscience. Although that change reduced the amount of cholesterol in the recipe, the calories and fat content per serving remained virtually unchanged. Butter and margarine are about equal in both calories and fat content. So the big reduction in both didn't occur until I replaced both the butter and margarine with Butter Buds. The result is a Stuffed Flounder that is lower in calories, fat content, and cholesterol content.

Traditional Recipe

1 pound flounder fillets (4 medium fillets)
½ cup chopped onions
½ cup chopped celery
⅔ cup water
8 tablespoons butter
1 cup toasted bread cubes or stuffing mix
1 tablespoon chopped fresh parsley
1 tablespoon chopped fresh basil
⅛ teaspoon garlic powder
salt and pepper to taste
4 tablespoons golden raisins
4 tablespoons butter (melted)
2 tablespoons white table wine
2 tablespoons lemon juice
sprinkle of paprika

Low-Fat Version

1 pound flounder fillets (4 medium fillets)
½ cup chopped onions
½ cup chopped celery
⅔ cup water
Butter Buds equivalent to 8 tablespoons butter
1 cup toasted bread cubes or stuffing mix (without tropical oils)
1 tablespoon chopped fresh parsley
1 tablespoon chopped fresh basil
⅛ teaspoon garlic powder
salt and pepper to taste
4 tablespoons golden raisins
Butter Buds equivalent to 4 tablespoons butter
2 tablespoons white table wine
2 tablespoons lemon juice
sprinkle of paprika

Wash flounder, pat dry, and set aside. Combine onions, celery, water, and butter in medium saucepan. Bring to a boil and simmer for 5–7 minutes. Remove from heat and add bread cubes, parsley, basil, garlic powder, salt, and pepper. Mix until all liquid is absorbed. (More·water may be added if a moister stuffing is desired.) Fold in raisins. Spoon stuffing mixture equally over flounder fillets. Roll fillets and place seam side down in a 9 × 13-inch glass baking dish. Combine remaining butter (melted), wine, and lemon juice and pour over fillets. Sprinkle with paprika and bake in 375° oven for 25 minutes. (Serves 4)

PER SERVING

Calories:	508
Fat:	37.8 grams
Cholesterol:	155 milligrams

Wash flounder, pat dry, and set aside. Combine onions, celery, water, and Butter Buds (equal to 8 tablespoons butter) in medium saucepan. Bring to a boil and simmer for 5–7 minutes. Remove from heat and add bread cubes, parsley, basil, garlic powder, salt, and pepper. Mix until all liquid is absorbed. (More water may be added if a moister stuffing is desired.) Fold in raisins. Spoon stuffing mixture equally over flounder fillets. Roll fillets and place seam side down in a 9 × 13-inch glass baking dish. Combine remaining Butter Buds (equal to 4 tablespoons butter), wine, and lemon juice and pour over fillets. Sprinkle with paprika and bake in 375° oven for 25 minutes. (Serves 4)

PER SERVING

Calories:	200
Fat:	1.5 grams
Cholesterol:	56 milligrams

Hawaiian Bay Scallops

If you enjoy seafood, but only indulge when dining out, you are not alone. Many people are intimidated by seafood because they underestimate their abilities in fish cookery. They are comfortable cooking a piece of chicken, a lamb chop, or a t-bone steak. Yet, when cooking a piece of fish, they succumb to such bland and boring methods of preparation that they have to bribe the kids to eat it! The word "fish" becomes synonymous with "tonic," or something we force ourselves to eat occasionally because "it's good for you."

There are, however, many interesting ways to prepare seafood; it is a great meal choice from a nutritional standpoint, and, because seafood requires so little cooking time, it is the ultimate entrée for people on the go.

The recipe for Hawaiian Bay Scallops is a terrific one for when you arrive home late and need to have a meal on the table in 15 minutes. Microwave a potato and toss a salad to accompany the scallops and dinner is served! Be careful, however, not to douse your seafood with added fats, or you will quickly offset its nutritional benefits. The original version of this scallop recipe calls for the use of butter and pine nuts. By eliminating the nuts and using a butter substitute in the revised recipe, I reduced the fat content per serving from almost 12 grams to less than 1 gram. At 140 calories per serving, this meal unquestionably qualifies as a superb choice for dieters. In fact, they can even afford to splurge with a double portion!

Traditional Recipe

1 tablespoon dry mustard
2 tablespoons pineapple juice
1 tablespoon lemon juice
2 tablespoons honey
2 tablespoons butter
1 pound bay scallops
¼ cup pine nuts

Low-Fat Version

Butter Buds equivalent to 4 tablespoons butter
1 tablespoon dry mustard
2 tablespoons pineapple juice
1 tablespoon lemon juice
2 tablespoons honey
1 pound bay scallops

In a cup or small bowl, dissolve dry mustard in a mixture of pineapple juice and lemon juice. Add honey and blend until smooth. Spoon mixture into a medium skillet. Add butter and heat until melted and ingredients are well-blended. Add scallops and toss until well-coated with honey mixture. Cook uncovered over medium heat about 6 minutes until liquid reduces and thickens and scallops are glazed, stirring constantly. Remove from heat. Add pine nuts and toss. (Serves 4)

Per Serving

Calories:	235
Fat:	11.8 grams
Cholesterol:	63 milligrams

In a cup or small bowl, dissolve dry Butter Buds and dry mustard in a mixture of pineapple juice and lemon juice. Add honey and blend until smooth. Spoon mixture into a medium, nonstick skillet and heat until mixture begins to bubble. Add scallops and toss until well-coated with honey mixture. Cook uncovered over medium-high heat about 6 minutes until liquid reduces and thickens and scallops are glazed, stirring constantly. (Serves 4)

Per Serving

Calories:	140
Fat:	0.9 gram
Cholesterol:	45 milligrams

🍒 Honey-Glazed Salmon

Fish of any type, prepared in the proper way, is an excellent choice for those on a heart-healthy dietary regime. Most varieties contain considerably less fat than red meat, and unlike most red meats, a higher percentage of the fat in fish is unsaturated, rather than saturated.

Methods of fish preparation are limited only by one's lack of imagination. I quickly discovered that there are many more exciting ways to prepare fish other than deep frying or baking with lemon butter. Years ago, fish was not a favorite meal choice in our house. Encouraging my family to eat more fish meant finding ways to disguise it, and so creating seafood recipes that offered both taste appeal and nutritional soundness became an ongoing challenge for me. I found that gourmet seafood dishes are often laced with rich sauces, making them unacceptable for individuals on low-fat diets. I began to experiment with these rich seafood recipes by making the necessary revisions or substitutions to create a defatted adaptation of the original. Such is the case with the Honey-Glazed Salmon recipe that follows. The original recipe turned a nutritious piece of salmon into a less than heart-healthy selection, attributable to a couple of high-fat villains—butter and almonds. In the revision, I replaced the butter with Butter Buds, and I eliminated the almonds. For those who miss the crunch provided by the almonds, some slivered water chestnuts can be sprinkled over the salmon just before serving.

Compare the food values at the end of each recipe. The numbers clearly show that the traditional version of this recipe completely reverses the nutritional benefits of a good piece of fish by including ingredients that transform it into a fat monster!

Traditional Recipe

1 pound salmon fillets
2 tablespoons honey
1 teaspoon dry mustard
2 tablespoons pineapple juice
1 tablespoon lemon juice
2 tablespoons melted butter
4 tablespoons slivered
  almonds

Low-Fat Version

1 pound salmon fillets
2 tablespoons honey
1 teaspoon dry mustard
2 tablespoons pineapple juice
1 tablespoon lemon juice
  Butter Buds equivalent to 2
  tablespoons butter
4 or 5 water chestnuts, cut into
  slivers (optional)

Arrange salmon fillets in shallow baking dish. Combine honey, mustard, pineapple juice, lemon juice, and butter. Blend thoroughly. Spoon mixture over salmon, coating entire surface of fish. Sprinkle with almonds. Bake in 400° oven for about 20 minutes, or until salmon flakes. Baste several times while baking, and thin glaze with a small amount of water if it becomes too thick or begins to stick. (Serves 4)

PER SERVING

Calories: 279
Fat: 14.9 grams
Cholesterol: 53 milligrams

Arrange salmon in shallow baking dish. Combine honey, mustard, pineapple juice, lemon juice, and Butter Buds. Blend thoroughly. Spoon mixture over salmon, coating entire surface of fish. Bake in 400° oven for about 20 minutes, or until salmon flakes. Baste several times while baking, and thin glaze with a small amount of water if it becomes too thick or begins to stick. If desired, sprinkle with slivered water chestnuts just before serving. (Serves 4)

PER SERVING

Calories: 185
Fat: 4.8 grams
Cholesterol: 35 milligrams

Food for Thought

"An ounce of willpower is worth a pound of fat."
—FRIAR TUCK

DESSERTS
AND
BREADS

Cream-Filled Fruit Tart

Rich cream desserts need not be written out of your life forever simply because you are committed to reducing dietary fat and cholesterol. The secret, of course, lies in preparation and choice of ingredients. Making thoughtful, low-fat substitutions for high-fat ingredients is the name of the game. Granted, some desserts lend themselves better to conversion than others, but almost all are worth a try.

Look at the following recipe for the Cream-Filled Fruit Tart, for example. At first glance, it appears a difficult task to adapt this recipe, primarily due to the use of shortening in the pastry. However, after settling on an alternate low-fat crust made with meringue, the remaining ingredients pose few problems. For the vanilla filling, a reduced-calorie pudding mix replaces the regular mix, and skim milk is used instead of whole milk, with minimal change in taste. The fruit topping and glaze require no revision at all.

Naturally, the revised version does not taste exactly the same as the original because of the difference in the two crusts. But, the filling and fruit are the dominant tastes in this dessert. Therefore, the absence of the original pastry is a small price to pay when you consider that you are enjoying a delicious creamy dessert, without betraying your low-fat, low-cholesterol commitment.

Traditional Recipe

⅔ cup flour
1 tablespoon sugar
3 tablespoons butter
2 tablespoons ice water
1 small box vanilla pudding mix (4-serving size)
2 cups milk
2 teaspoons sugar
1 teaspoon cornstarch
½ cup pineapple juice
1 kiwi fruit, peeled and sliced
1 banana, thinly sliced
6 large strawberries, thinly sliced

To make crust, combine flour and sugar. Cut in butter until mixture resembles coarse crumbs. Sprinkle ice water over crumbs and toss until crumbs begin to adhere. Form into a ball. Roll dough out between two pieces of waxed paper, until it is about 10 inches in diameter. Transfer pastry onto an ungreased baking sheet or pizza pan. Crimp edge with fingers or fork, and bake at 400° for 12 minutes, or until lightly browned. Remove from oven and cool. Transfer to serving plate.

For the filling, combine pudding mix and milk and prepare according to package directions. Cool for about 10 minutes, and stir 2 or 3 times while cooling. Spoon filling evenly onto pastry shell. Chill in refrigerator until well-set.

To prepare glaze, combine 2 teaspoons sugar and cornstarch in a small saucepan. Stir in pineapple juice. Heat and stir until thick and bubbly. Set aside to cool.

Meanwhile, arrange fruit slices on top of chilled filling in the following manner, overlapping fruit slices as they are arranged: Kiwi in center, banana slices around kiwi, and strawberry slices around banana. Spoon glaze over fruit and chill tart thoroughly before serving. (Serves 8)

Per Serving

Calories:	273
Fat:	9.2 grams
Cholesterol:	29 milligrams

Low-Fat Version

2 egg whites
¼ teaspoon vanilla
3 tablespoons sugar
1 small box low-calorie
   vanilla pudding mix
   (4-serving size)
2 cups skim milk
2 teaspoons sugar
1 teaspoon cornstarch
½ cup pineapple juice
1 kiwi fruit, peeled and
   sliced
1 banana, thinly sliced
6 large strawberries, thinly
   sliced

To make the meringue crust, beat egg whites and vanilla with electric beater until soft peaks are formed. Gradually add sugar and continue beating until stiff peaks are formed. Spoon meringue into nonstick 9-inch pie plate. Using the back of a soup spoon, spread meringue so it covers entire bottom and sides of pie plate. Bake in 300° oven for about 40 minutes, or until crust is dry and lightly browned. Remove from oven and set aside to cool.

For the filling, combine pudding mix and milk and prepare according to package directions. Cool slightly and pour into meringue shell. Chill in refrigerator until well-set.

To prepare glaze, combine 2 teaspoons sugar and cornstarch in a small saucepan. Stir in pineapple juice. Heat and stir until thick and bubbly. Set aside to cool.

Meanwhile, arrange fruit slices on top of chilled filling in following manner, overlapping fruit slices as they are arranged: Kiwi in center, banana slices around kiwi, and strawberry slices around banana. Spoon glaze over fruit and chill tart thoroughly before serving. (Serves 8)

Per Serving

Calories:	126
Fat:	0.3 gram
Cholesterol:	1 milligram

🍓 Strawberry Fluff

Beginning a low-fat, low-cholesterol dietary regime may seem a simple task for a highly-motivated individual, but remaining motivated and staying on the diet indefinitely is quite another story.

Encouraging the support of other family members often helps. If a spouse and children become involved in a newly discovered healthy dietary regime, it will encourage the individual to remain on course and thereby prevent potential problems. At the same time, getting the family committed to a healthier diet is a giant step toward reducing the health risks associated with poor nutritional habits.

How can we accomplish this last step? How do we convince our children of the merits of healthy eating habits? Answer: We lure them in by demonstrating that low-fat foods can taste good. Creating taste-tempting desserts can provide that special magic.

There are many traditional desserts that can be converted to acceptable low-fat treats by a few substitutions, such as cheesecakes, cream pies, and pudding or Jell-O desserts. The following recipe for Strawberry Fluff is a simple dessert that tastes as good in the low-fat version as in the original. By replacing the sour cream with nonfat yogurt, I converted it to a low-calorie, low-fat, low-cholesterol dessert.

Remember, with a little creativity, friends should not feel sorry for you just because you're pursuing a low-fat life style. In fact, why not invite them to a delicious low-fat dinner that might convince them to join you!

Traditional Recipe

1 3½-ounce box strawberry Jell-O
¾ cup hot water
1 cup ice cubes covered with water
1 cup sour cream
½ teaspoon vanilla
1 cup sliced strawberries
extra strawberries for garnish (optional)

Low-Fat Version

1 3½-ounce box strawberry Jell-O
¾ cup hot water
1 cup ice cubes covered with water
1 cup plain nonfat yogurt
½ teaspoon vanilla
1 cup sliced strawberries
extra strawberries for garnish (optional)

Dissolve Jell-O in hot water. Place in blender on low speed for 1 minute. Add ice cubes and water, and blend until smooth. Add sour cream and vanilla, and blend for about 40 seconds longer. Set out 8 parfait glasses. Divide strawberry slices equally among the 8 glasses. Pour Jell-O mixture over strawberries and refrigerate until well-set. If desired, garnish with additional strawberry slices on top of each dessert before serving. (Serves 8)

PER SERVING

Calories:	114
Fat:	6 grams
Cholesterol:	11 milligrams

Dissolve Jell-O in hot water. Place in blender on low speed for 1 minute. Add ice cubes and water, and blend until smooth. Add yogurt and vanilla, and blend for about 40 seconds longer. Set out 8 parfait glasses. Divide strawberry slices equally among the 8 glasses. Pour Jell-O mixture over strawberries and refrigerate until well-set. If desired, garnish with additional strawberry slices on top of each dessert before serving. (Serves 8)

PER SERVING

Calories:	60
Fat:	none
Cholesterol:	less than 1 milligram

 **Bread Pudding**

I revised the original recipe for Bread Pudding for a friend whose husband required a low-fat, low-cholesterol diet due to a recent heart ailment. I happened to be visiting her home at a time when she was serving bread pudding for dessert. Feeling very guilty by my presence, she quickly commented that it was not customary for her to serve bread pudding for dessert, but as a special treat to her husband on Father's Day, she deviated slightly from routine and served his favorite dessert.

I suggested that she let me look at her recipe to see what changes I could make to render the recipe an acceptable low-fat dessert. A quick glance revealed that the recipe was a cinch to convert! I replaced the whole milk and eggs in the original recipe with skim milk and egg substitute. To reduce the fat and calories further, I substituted bread cubes from "lite" bread for regular enriched white bread. Most "lite" breads are made without shortening, but be sure to verify this by reading ingredients on package labels before purchasing.

To reduce calories a bit more, I cut back on the amount of sugar and raisins used in the original recipe. I felt my friend's bread pudding was too sweet, anyway.

These few changes were simple to carry out and effectively lowered the calories, fat, and cholesterol content of each serving. Moreover, the quality of taste was virtually unchanged. But, most important, the changes permitted the return of her husband's favorite dessert to the dinner table without the guilt!

Traditional Recipe

2 cups milk
1/2 cup sugar
2 eggs, beaten
1 teaspoon vanilla
1/2 teaspoon cinnamon
1/8 teaspoon salt
2 1/4 cups bread cubes from day old white bread
1/3 cup dark seedless raisins

Low-Fat Version

2 cups skim milk
1/3 cup sugar
egg substitute equivalent to 2 eggs
1 teaspoon vanilla
1/2 teaspoon cinnamon
1/8 teaspoon salt (optional)
2 1/4 cups bread cubes from day old "lite" bread
1/4 cup dark seedless raisins

In a large bowl, combine milk, sugar, eggs, vanilla, cinnamon, and salt. Stir in bread cubes and raisins. Spoon mixture evenly into 6 custard cups. Set cups into a pan of hot water about 1-inch deep. Bake at 350° for about 35 minutes, or until toothpick or knife inserted into center of pudding comes out clean. (Serves 6)

PER SERVING

Calories:	208
Fat:	5.1 grams
Cholesterol:	82 milligrams

In a large bowl, combine skim milk, sugar, egg substitute, vanilla, cinnamon, and salt. Stir in bread cubes and raisins. Spoon mixture evenly into 6 custard cups. Set custard cups into a pan of hot water about 1-inch deep. Bake at 350° for about 35 minutes, or until toothpick or knife inserted into center of pudding comes out clean. (Serves 6)

PER SERVING

Calories:	121
Fat:	0.3 gram
Cholesterol:	1 milligram

🍒 Rice Pudding

Rice Pudding has always been an old standard when it comes to tried and true American desserts. It was a favorite in our home when I was a child. We had it once or twice a week because my mother insisted it was an easy way to help supplement our dairy requirements. Of course, in those days no one seemed concerned about the amount of fat in the diet, and the word "cholesterol" was not even a part of our vocabulary. Naturally, one would not even consider making rice pudding with anything but farm fresh eggs and rich whole milk. Today, however, as a health-conscious adult I realize the risks associated with too much dietary fat and cholesterol, so I make every effort to reduce my intake of both whenever possible. By making two simple substitutions, I turned my mother's original Rice Pudding recipe into a delicious low-fat treat. In fact, according to my family the taste remains unchanged. Compare the nutrient values of both versions of Rice Pudding shown below. Then, try the low-fat version for your family, and you will never make the traditional recipe again!

Traditional Recipe

⅓ cup uncooked long grain rice
¼ cup water
2 cups whole milk
2 tablespoons sugar
⅛ teaspoon salt
1 egg, slightly beaten
1 teaspoon vanilla extract
¼ cup raisins
   cinnamon to taste

Low-Fat Version

⅓ cup uncooked long grain rice
¼ cup water
2 cups skim milk
2 tablespoons sugar
⅛ teaspoon salt
   egg substitute equivalent to 1 egg
1 teaspoon vanilla extract
¼ cup raisins
   cinnamon to taste

Combine rice, water, 1½ cups milk, sugar, and salt in saucepan. Bring to a boil while stirring constantly. Reduce heat, cover, and simmer for about 25 minutes, or until rice is tender. Combine remaining milk, egg, and vanilla and beat slightly. Add to cooked rice and continue cooking over low heat about 10 more minutes until thick and creamy. .Fold in raisins. Spoon into dessert dishes and sprinkle with cinnamon. Chill. (Serves 4)

PER SERVING

Calories: 195
Fat: 5.5 grams
Cholesterol: 70 milligrams

Combine rice, water, 1½ cups skim milk, sugar, and salt in saucepan. Bring to a boil while stirring constantly. Reduce heat, cover, and simmer about 25 minutes, or until rice is tender. Combine remaining skim milk, egg substitute, and vanilla and beat slightly. Add to cooked rice and continue cooking over low heat about 10 more minutes until thick and creamy. Fold in raisins. Spoon into dessert dishes and sprinkle with cinnamon. Chill. (Serves 4)

PER SERVING

Calories: 153
Fat: 0.2 gram
Cholesterol: 2 milligrams

 # Crème Caramel

Crème Caramel, or caramel custard, is a dessert with international appeal. It can be found on the menu of most fine restaurants from the world famous Maxim's in Paris, to the equally famous Hugo's in Singapore.

In its traditional form, this light custard is prepared with eggs and whole milk, which are the only sources of cholesterol and fat in the recipe. Thus, by using non-cholesterol egg substitute and skim milk as replacements, I have eliminated the culprits. Happily, I did not eliminate the light texture or good taste with these substitutions.

Compare the food values in the recipes for both traditional and low-fat, low-cholesterol Crème Caramel. Then try the heart-healthy version and you will discover that it is an excellent replacement for the original recipe. When you consider the fat and cholesterol content of each, the revised version is the clear-cut winner on all counts!

Traditional Recipe

4 eggs
9 tablespoons sugar
1 teaspoon vanilla extract
4 cups warm milk
1 teaspoon lemon juice

Low-Fat Version

egg substitute equivalent to 4 eggs
9 tablespoons sugar
1 teaspoon vanilla extract
4 cups warm skim milk
1 teaspoon lemon juice

In a medium mixing bowl, beat eggs, 4 tablespoons sugar, and vanilla on low speed with electric mixer. Gradually add warm milk, and continue beating on low speed until well-blended. Set aside. Place remaining 5 tablespoons of sugar and lemon juice in a small saucepan over low heat. Cook, stirring constantly, until sugar begins to caramelize (become brown and foamy). Set out 8 custard cups and spoon equal amounts of caramelized sugar into each cup. Rotate cups to coat sides with sugar. Pour custard over caramelized sugar, dividing custard equally among the 8 cups. Place cups in a large pan containing about 1 inch of hot water. Place in 325° oven and bake for 35–40 minutes, or until toothpick inserted in the center of cup comes out clean. Remove from oven and cool. Refrigerate until thoroughly chilled before serving. (Serves 8)

Per Serving

Calories:	167
Fat:	6.9 grams
Cholesterol:	123 milligrams

In a medium mixing bowl, beat egg substitute, 4 tablespoons sugar, and vanilla on low speed with electric mixer. Gradually add warm milk, and continue beating on low speed until well-blended. Set aside. Place remaining 5 tablespoons sugar and lemon juice in a small saucepan over low heat. Cook, stirring constantly, until sugar begins to caramelize (become brown and foamy). Set out 8 custard cups and spoon equal amounts of caramelized sugar into each cup. Rotate cups to coat sides with sugar. Pour custard over caramelized sugar, dividing custard equally among the 8 cups. Place cups in a large pan containing about 1 inch of hot water. Place in 325° oven and bake for 35–40 minutes, or until toothpick inserted in the center of cup comes out clean. Remove from oven and cool. Refrigerate until thoroughly chilled before serving. (Serves 8)

Per Serving

Calories:	113
Fat:	less than 1 gram
Cholesterol:	2 milligrams

🍎 Apple Crumb Pie

Apple pie was the dessert we craved most after embarking on a low-fat, low-cholesterol diet. It wasn't long, however, before I discovered a way to put apple pie back on our dinner table.

Naturally, my new creation is a revised version of our old favorite, but the taste is reminiscent of the old standard and satisfying enough that we no longer feel deprived. The most significant change made in the new recipe is the elimination of the bottom crust and the subsequent elimination of about half the calories and fat. Both are reduced even further when the butter in the crumb topping is replaced with Butter Buds and Karo syrup. I reduced the quantity of sugar and flour in the revised recipe. Reducing the sugar actually improves the taste!

Note that I have allowed for larger portions of the low-fat pie, because without a crust it is less filling. Of course, there are some disadvantages to a crustless pie. For example, the slice of pie tends to lose its wedge shape when served because there is no crust to give it form. Although the shape is altered, the taste is not impaired one iota! Moreover, when you compare the nutritional values of each, especially the fat content, I guarantee that you will gladly trade a slightly offbeat shape for the nutritional gain. It is a small price to pay for the taste of apple pie without the guilt!

Traditional Recipe

6 medium apples (pared, cored, and thinly sliced)
1 tablespoon lemon juice
1 9-inch unbaked pastry shell (frozen variety is fine)
½ cup sugar
½ teaspoon cinnamon
⅓ cup sugar
¾ cup flour
6 tablespoons butter

No-Crust Low-Fat Version

6 medium apples (pared, cored, and thinly sliced)
1 tablespoon lemon juice
¼ cup white sugar
½ cup flour
¼ cup brown sugar
Butter Buds equivalent to 4 tablespoons butter
½ teaspoon cinnamon
1 tablespoon Karo syrup (light corn syrup)

Toss apples with lemon juice and arrange in unbaked pie shell. Combine ½ cup sugar and cinnamon. Sprinkle over apples. Mix ⅓ cup sugar with flour. Cut in butter until mixture is crumbly. Sprinkle crumbs over apples. Bake at 400° for 35 minutes or until crumbs are brown. Serve warm or cold. (Serves 8)

PER SERVING

Calories:	370
Fat:	21.5 grams
Cholesterol:	27 milligrams

Combine apples, lemon juice, and white sugar. Toss well and spoon into 9-inch, deep-dish pie plate. Place into 375° oven for 10 minutes. Meanwhile, combine flour, brown sugar, Butter Buds, cinnamon, and Karo syrup. Mix with fork until slightly crumblike in texture. Remove apples from oven and fold about two-thirds of the crumb mixture into the apples. Sprinkle remaining crumbs on top of apples. Return pie to oven and bake for about 30 minutes until brown and bubbly. Serve warm or cold. (Serves 6)

PER SERVING

Calories:	198
Fat:	less than 1 gram
Cholesterol:	none

🍎 Pumpkin Cheesecake

A Pumpkin Cheesecake recipe in both the original and heart-healthy versions follows. Each version has been analyzed for calorie, fat, and cholesterol content. It is obvious that a few simple substitutions result in a heart-healthy Pumpkin Cheesecake with significantly lower calorie, fat, and cholesterol content. The best part . . . it tastes great.

Traditional Recipe

2½ cups ricotta cheese, cream style
1 cup canned pumpkin
½ cup granulated light brown sugar
2 eggs
1½ teaspoons vanilla
½ teaspoon allspice
½ teaspoon cinnamon
¼ teaspoon ginger

Low-Fat Version

2½ cups lowfat cottage cheese (1% or less)
1 cup canned pumpkin
½ cup granulated light brown sugar
egg substitute equivalent to 2 eggs
1½ teaspoons vanilla
½ teaspoon allspice
½ teaspoon cinnamon
¼ teaspoon ginger

Combine ricotta cheese and pumpkin and mix thoroughly. Add all other ingredients and blend well. Pour into lightly greased 10-inch spring-form pan and bake at 325° for 1 hour. Turn oven off and allow cheesecake to remain in oven for about 45 minutes to set. Remove cake from oven. Cool for 15 minutes; then chill thoroughly in refrigerator before serving. (Serves 12)

Per Serving

Calories:	143
Fat:	7.7 grams
Cholesterol:	62 milligrams

Process cottage cheese in food processor or blender until smooth. Add pumpkin and mix thoroughly. Add all other ingredients and blend well. Pour into ungreased 10-inch springform pan and bake at 325° for 1 hour. Turn oven off and allow cheesecake to remain in oven for about 45 minutes to set. Remove cake from oven. Cool for 15 minutes; then chill thoroughly in refrigerator before serving. (Serves 12)

Per Serving

Calories:	80
Fat:	less than 1 gram
Cholesterol:	2 milligrams

Chocolate Meringue Pie

Absolutely not! People on heart-healthy diets can not eat rich pies—or *can* they? If you are seriously making an effort to reduce the amount of fat and cholesterol you consume, you should scrutinize labels on commercially made baked goods before placing them in your grocery cart. Most baked goods, especially those made with pastry dough, contain generous amounts of shortening, making them high in fat content.

So what can you do when your sweet tooth beckons? Learn to make a pie crust without shortening, and you will be able to satisfy that craving with a home-baked pie.

Two recipes for Chocolate Meringue Pie follow. In the low-fat version, cornflake crumbs are substituted for graham cracker crumbs because unlike graham cracker crumbs they contain no added fat. Additionally, Butter Buds replaces butter and skim milk replaces whole milk.

Now who said you can't have pie? Check the reduced calories, fat, and cholesterol in the revised recipe and start baking!

Traditional Recipe

PIE SHELL
- 1¼ cups graham cracker crumbs
- ¼ cup sugar
- 6 tablespoons butter, melted

FILLING
- ½ cup sugar
- 2 tablespoons cornstarch
- 2 tablespoons cocoa powder
- ½ teaspoon salt
- 2 cups whole milk

MERINGUE
- 2 egg whites
- 2 tablespoons sugar

To make the pie shell combine graham cracker crumbs, sugar and melted butter and mix. Press crumbs into 9-inch pie plate, covering bottom and sides. Bake at 375° for about 8 minutes or until edges are brown. Remove from oven and set aside to cool.

To make the filling, combine the sugar, cornstarch, cocoa, and salt in a medium saucepan. Gradually stir in milk and cook over medium heat until mixture boils. Continue boiling for 1 or 2 minutes until mixture begins to thicken, stirring constantly. Remove from heat and cool for 5 minutes. Pour into baked pie shell. Set pie aside to cool and set.

To prepare the meringue, place egg whites in medium mixing bowl and beat with an electric mixer until frothy. Gradually add sugar and continue beating on high speed until meringue forms stiff peaks. Spread meringue over pie, making sure to cover all the filling. Place pie in 400° oven for about 10 minutes, or until meringue is lightly golden. Remove from oven and cool. Refrigerate thoroughly before serving. (Serves 10)

PER SERVING

Calories: 202
Fat: 10.3 grams
Cholesterol: 34 milligrams

Low-Fat Version

PIE SHELL
1 cup nonfat cornflake
  crumbs
  Butter Buds equivalent to 4
  tablespoons butter
3 tablespoons frozen apple
  juice concentrate,
  thawed and undiluted

FILLING
$\frac{1}{2}$ cup sugar
2 tablespoons cornstarch
2 tablespoons cocoa powder
$\frac{1}{2}$ teaspoon salt
2 cups skim milk

MERINGUE
2 egg whites
2 tablespoons sugar

To make the pie shell, place cornflake crumbs and Butter Buds in medium bowl and sprinkle with apple juice concentrate. Blend with fork. Press crumbs into 9-inch pie plate, covering bottom and sides. Bake at 400° for 12 minutes, or until crust is brown. Remove from oven and set aside to cool.

To make the filling, combine the sugar, cornstarch, cocoa, and salt in a medium saucepan. Gradually stir in milk and cook over medium heat until mixture boils. Continue boiling for about 1 or 2 minutes, until mixture begins to thicken, stirring constantly. Remove from heat and cool for 5 minutes. Pour into baked pie shell. Set pie aside to cool and set.

To prepare the meringue, place egg whites in medium mixing bowl and beat with an electric mixer until frothy. Gradually add the sugar and continue beating on high speed until meringue forms stiff peaks. Spread meringue over pie, making sure to cover all the filling. Place pie in 400° oven for about 10 minutes, or until meringue is lightly golden. Remove from oven and cool. Refrigerate thoroughly before serving. (Serves 10)

PER SERVING

Calories:	110
Fat:	0.4 gram
Cholesterol:	1 milligram

🍓 *Strawberry and Cream Crêpes*

A low-fat diet is not a fate worse than death. It need not be bland or boring, nor does it mean that your lips will never again touch a "real" dessert.

As you can see from the following recipes, with appropriate substitutions, even rich creamy dessert recipes can be modified to accommodate dieters or health-conscious individuals who are striving to reduce the amount of fat and cholesterol in their diets.

This Strawberry and Cream Crêpes recipe required a minimal amount of modification to convert it to an acceptable low-fat dessert. Yet, the savings in calories, fat, and cholesterol is rather significant. As far as taste is concerned, the low-fat version comes very close to the traditional version. It is a real treat, especially for people on low-fat diets who thought that they were doomed forever to angel food cake and fruit as their daily desserts!

Traditional Recipe

CRÊPES
1 egg
½ cup flour
½ teaspoon sugar
½ cup whole milk

FILLING
1 cup whole milk ricotta cheese
3 tablespoons sugar
1 teaspoon vanilla extract
2 cups sliced strawberries

To make the crêpes, place egg in medium bowl. Beat slightly. Add flour and sugar, mixing well. Add milk gradually and beat with a whisk or electric beater until batter is smooth. Heat 7-inch crêpe pan or nonstick skillet. Pour in 2 to 3 tablespoons of batter, then lift pan above the heating unit and tilt in all directions, allowing batter to coat bottom of pan. (This must be done quickly, before batter sets.) Return pan to heating unit and cook on medium heat until lightly browned on bottom and dry on top. Carefully loosen edges of crêpe and flip it over. Cook on opposite side for about 20 seconds. Remove crêpe from pan and place on paper towel to cool. Repeat until all batter has been used up. Makes about 8 crêpes.

For the filling, combine ricotta cheese, sugar, and vanilla and whip with electric mixer until smooth and creamy. Fold in strawberries. Place a crêpe on plate and spoon filling along center of crêpe. Fold one side of the crêpe over filling. Then fold over the other side, so that it overlaps the first. Fill remaining crêpes in the same manner. Serve immediately or chill until ready to serve. (Serves 8)

PER SERVING

Calories:	132
Fat:	5.4 grams
Cholesterol:	45 milligrams

Strawberry and Cream Crêpes

(continued)

Low-Fat Version

CRÊPES

egg substitute equivalent to
1 egg
½ cup flour
½ teaspoon sugar
½ cup skim milk

FILLING

1 cup low-fat cottage cheese
(1% or less)
3 tablespoons sugar
1 teaspoon vanilla extract
2 cups sliced strawberries

To make the crêpes, place egg substitute in medium bowl. Add flour and sugar, mixing well. Add milk gradually and beat with a whisk or electric beater until batter is smooth. Heat 7-inch crêpe pan or nonstick skillet. Pour in 2 to 3 tablespoons of batter, then lift pan above the heating unit and tilt in all directions, allowing batter to coat bottom of pan. (This must be done quickly, before batter sets.) Return pan to heating unit and cook on medium heat until lightly browned on bottom and dry on top. Carefully loosen edges of crêpe and flip it over. Cook on opposite side for about 20 seconds. Remove crêpe from pan and place on paper towel to cool. Repeat until all batter has been used up. Makes about 8 crêpes.

For the filling, combine cottage cheese, sugar, and vanilla and whip with electric mixer until smooth and creamy. Fold in strawberries. Place a crêpe on plate and spoon filling along center of crêpe. Fold one side of the crêpe over filling. Then fold over the other side, so that it overlaps the first. Fill remaining crêpes in same manner. Serve immediately or chill until ready to serve. (Serves 8)

Per Serving

Calories: 84
Fat: 0.4 gram
Cholesterol: 2 milligrams

Carrot Bread

"Eat your carrots" was a familiar phrase at the dinner table when I was a child. It was usually followed with, "they're good for your eyes." Fact is, neither statement had much impact on my eating habits. I never cared much for carrots. Consequently, they usually remained firmly planted on my plate until after-dinner clean-up began. Occasionally I moved them around on the dish, hiding a few slices under some mashed potatoes or lettuce leaves to make it appear as if I had eaten some.

Today, however, carrots are among my favorites. I enjoy them raw, cooked, in soups, stews, or in any number of other ways. Not only are carrots one of the most flavorful and economical vegetables to prepare, they are also a wonderful source of carotene—a form of vitamin A that has been recommended for its cancer prevention potential. Additionally, carrots are essentially fat-free and are high in soluble fiber, which some authorities suggest has cholesterol-lowering benefits.

I doubt that any of this nutritional information will impress you much if you dislike carrots. However, it may nudge you just enough to try the following recipe for Carrot Bread.

In order to reduce the calories, fat, and cholesterol some changes were made in the original recipe. These changes included a reduction in the amount of sugar, the use of egg substitute, the elimination of vegetable oil and chopped walnuts, and the addition of raisins. The resulting low-fat version of Carrot Bread has about half the calories per serving and is virtually fat-free! Even if carrots are not among your favorites, try this one. You will never even know you are eating carrots!

Traditional Recipe

1½ cups shredded carrots
½ cup brown sugar
½ cup white sugar
1 teaspoon baking soda
2 tablespoons vegetable oil
1 cup boiling water
2 eggs, slightly beaten
2⅓ cups all-purpose flour
2½ teaspoons baking powder
1 teaspoon salt
⅛ teaspoon ground nutmeg
1 cup chopped walnuts

Low-Fat Version

1½ cups shredded carrots
½ cup brown sugar
¼ cup granulated white sugar
1 teaspoon baking soda
1 cup boiling water
egg substitute equivalent to 2 eggs
2⅓ cups unbleached flour
2½ teaspoons baking powder
1 teaspoon salt
⅛ teaspoon ground nutmeg
⅔ cup dark raisins

Combine carrots, sugars, baking soda, and oil in large mixing bowl, mixing well. Gradually stir in boiling water. Set aside to cool. When mixture is cool, add eggs and blend. In separate bowl combine flour, baking powder, salt, and nutmeg. Stir these dry ingredients gradually into carrot mixture. Fold in walnuts. Pour batter into well-greased 9 × 5-inch loaf pan. Bake in 350° oven for 50–60 minutes, or until toothpick inserted into center of loaf comes out clean. Cool slightly. Remove from pan and place on wire rack to cool thoroughly. Wrap in plastic wrap and store at room temperature to retain moistness. (Serves 18)

Per Serving

Calories:	202
Fat:	7 grams
Cholesterol:	24 milligrams

Combine carrots, sugars, and baking soda in large bowl, mixing well. Gradually stir in boiling water. Set aside to cool. When cool stir in egg substitute. In separate bowl combine flour, baking powder, salt, and nutmeg. Add these dry ingredients gradually to carrot mixture, blending well after each addition. Fold in raisins. Pour batter into nonstick 9 × 5-inch loaf pan, or a pan sprayed very lightly with a nonstick vegetable oil spray. Bake in 350° oven for 50–60 minutes, or until toothpick inserted into center of loaf comes out clean. Cool slightly. Remove from pan and place on wire rack to cool thoroughly. Wrap in plastic wrap and store at room temperature to retain moistness. (Serves 18)

Per Serving

Calories:	110
Fat:	less than 1 gram
Cholesterol:	none

Corn Bread

Bread, of any kind, has always been one of my weaknesses. Fortunately, low-fat diets generally advocate generous amounts of complex carbohydrates daily, such as grain products—a suggestion that I find very appealing.

You may think that since a program of weight control is an inherent part of a healthy life style, you should not load up on breads and other starchy foods. Although it is true that overindulging on carbohydrates can cause the calories to mount, it is the fat in our diet that is responsible for most of the fat on our bodies. A gram of carbohydrate (bread, pasta, rice, potato, etc.) has about 4 calories. A gram of fat, on the other hand, has 9 calories—more than twice that of carbohydrates. Moreover, carbohydrates eaten in moderation are generally burned off in the form of energy exerted. The excess fat we eat, however, usually is stored in the body in the form of fat. So, anyone on a serious weight control program should be more concerned with reducing fat calories, rather than carbohydrate calories.

Two versions of a recipe for Corn Bread follow. As you can see, it is the fat in the original version that drives up the calorie count. Once I eliminate the shortening and whole milk, a serving falls in line with a serving of ordinary bread. So, if you love corn bread, don't deprive yourself. Simply make a few adjustments to the recipe, as shown in the low-fat version, and enjoy a piece without feeling guilty!

Traditional Recipe

1 cup corn meal
1 cup all-purpose flour
3 tablespoons sugar
1 tablespoon baking powder
1/4 teaspoon salt
1/4 cup oil
1 cup milk
2 eggs, slightly beaten

Low-Fat Version

1 cup corn meal
1 cup unbleached flour
3 tablespoons sugar
2 teaspoons baking powder
1 teaspoon baking soda
1/4 teaspoon salt
1/2 cup plain nonfat yogurt
1/2 cup skim milk
3 egg whites, beaten until frothy

Combine all dry ingredients in a medium bowl. Stir in oil, milk, and eggs and blend until all dry ingredients are moistened. Do not over beat. Pour into an 8-inch square well-greased baking pan. Bake in 400° oven for 20–25 minutes. (Serves 16)

PER SERVING

Calories:	118
Fat:	4.8 grams
Cholesterol:	29 milligrams

Combine all dry ingredients in a medium mixing bowl. Stir in yogurt, milk, and egg whites until dry ingredients are moistened. Pour into nonstick 8-inch square baking pan. Bake in 400° oven for 20–25 minutes. (Serves 16)

PER SERVING

Calories:	78
Fat:	0.2 gram
Cholesterol:	less than 1 milligram

🐦 Recipe Conversion Tips

The operative word in this book is "convert." Fad diets that rely on radical changes in one's normal dietary routine, either with foods that are strange to one's life style or gimmicky, are short-lived. A diet based on deprivation is a diet that is eventually bound to fail.

It takes years to develop eating habits, food preferences, and life style. It is difficult, if not impossible, to expect a total about-face with regard to food choices when the need for a change in eating habits becomes apparent.

Accordingly, my philosophy is that, within reason, you should not be compelled to "give up" the taste and enjoyment of the foods you learned to appreciate over the years. Rather, you simply need to renovate or convert your favorite dishes to fit the criteria of your new eating program. In the case of a low-fat, low-cholesterol life style, often the substitution of one ingredient in a recipe can turn a fat-laden meal into a heart-healthy one—without loss of taste.

Here are some tips for converting your favorite recipes to create your very own low-fat, low-cholesterol versions:

1. Begin with nonstick cookware, baking pans, and casseroles in order to eliminate the need for added fats to prevent sticking.
2. In place of red meat, choose fish and poultry more frequently.
3. Use chicken and turkey breast cutlets in recipes calling for thinly sliced veal, beef, pork, or lamb.
4. Use turkey thigh meat for stews, stroganoff, or in any recipe where a "dark" meat seems more appropriate for the visual appeal of the recipe.
5. Use ground turkey or chicken (without fat or skin added) in place of ground red meat.
6. Choose the following turkey products in place of their red meat counterparts: turkey pastrami, turkey sausage (no fat or skin added), turkey ham, turkey bacon, turkey kielbasa, and so on. (Caution: These

processed poultry products should be used sparingly, however, because most contain substantial quantities of sodium and more liberal amounts of fat than unprocessed turkey or chicken.)

7. Choose low-fat dairy products as follows:
   a. Skim milk for whole milk.
   b. Evaporated skim milk for light cream. (Add some nonfat powdered milk to the evaporated skim milk for an even richer texture similar to heavy cream.)
   c. Dry curd cottage cheese, 1 percent cottage cheese, or fully skim ricotta in place of whole milk ricotta cheese.
   d. Nonfat yogurt instead of whole milk yogurt.
   e. Nonfat plain yogurt that has been drained in refrigerator overnight in a strainer lined with paper towels in place of cream cheese. This is called "yogurt cheese."
   f. "Fat-free" or skim milk cheese products in place of regular high-fat cheese products.
   g. Nonfat frozen yogurt instead of ice cream.
   h. Low-fat sour cream in place of ordinary sour cream. (To prepare your own low-fat sour cream, place 1 cup of 1 percent cottage cheese, ¼ cup nonfat plain yogurt, and 1 tablespoon white vinegar into a blender or food processor and blend for a minute or two until smooth.)
8. Use Butter Buds nonfat natural butter flavoring in place of butter or margarine.
9. Make defatted stock for soups, sauces, and gravies by refrigerating poultry stock overnight and skimming off layer of fat that congeals on surface of broth.
10. In place of oil for sautéing, use wine, defatted poultry or fish stock, vegetable stock, or fruit juice.
11. Use non-cholesterol egg substitute or egg whites in place of whole eggs. (Two egg whites equals one whole egg.)
12. Replace regular salad dressings with commercially prepared non-oil, fat-free salad dressings.
13. Use commercial liquid smoke flavoring in recipes where "smokehouse" flavoring is desired. (Normally, this flavor is obtained by using high-fat smoked meat products.)
14. Instead of deep frying, bread and bake, or bread and broil on a nonstick cookie sheet.
15. Use generous quantities of fresh and dried herbs, along with a dash or two of lemon juice to provide added flavor and to compensate for the reduction of salt in recipes.

🍒 *Tips on Dining Out*

While one is always able to get three well-balanced, nutritious meals at home, what happens when you eat out at a diner, cafeteria, or restaurant?

Here are some simple, basic guidelines to follow:

1. Choose restaurants that offer low-fat, low-cholesterol choices whenever possible.
2. For breakfast, consider an omelet with non-cholesterol egg substitute, or egg whites, and low-fat ingredients, such as mushrooms, green peppers, and onions.
3. Enjoy an occasional stack of pancakes, but omit the dollop of butter and use only the syrup.
4. If you're a "cereal and fruit" person, remember to request skim or low-fat milk for the cereal.
5. Preserves, honey, or jelly should be your spread of choice for your toast or bagel, instead of butter or margarine.
6. Always choose pita bread, English muffins, and bagels (preferably NOT egg bagels) instead of enriched breads, rolls, danish, and muffins.
7. For lunch, select sliced turkey or chicken breast with lettuce and tomato as a sandwich filler, instead of high-fat luncheon meats and cheeses.
8. Treat yourself, anytime, to a vegetarian pizza (lots of veggies, but no cheese!).
9. Be very selective at the salad bar or buffet table. Do not be deceived by prepared salads. Often they are heavily laden with fat, in the form of mayonnaise or salad dressing.
10. Avoid high-fat red meats as much as possible and select poultry or fish dishes that have been broiled or baked without added sauces— unless you ask about the ingredients in the sauce and you are satisfied with the answer.

11. Avoid all foods that are deep-fried in fat.
12. Be cautious of terms such as "broiled in a garlic butter sauce" or "baked in a creamy wine sauce." Request that that food be baked or broiled with lemon juice or wine instead of butter.
13. Consider a stir-fried seafood, or chicken and vegetable dinner and specify that a small amount of fruit juice or white wine be used for frying instead of oil.
14. Select a pasta dinner with a plain tomato sauce or a seafood sauce, such as linguini with clam sauce. Often these are made to order and you can ask that they eliminate the added oil normally used in preparation.
15. Avoid meals that contain high-fat cheeses and cheese sauces.
16. When ordering a broiled combination seafood dinner, ask that it be served with some lemon wedges and a side dish of cocktail sauce, instead of the usual melted butter.
17. Be prepared. Carry a packet of Butter Buds nonfat butter flavoring with you and ask the waitress to bring you some hot water and a small bowl or cup to dissolve the flavoring for use on your baked potato, lobster, and so on.
18. To dress your salad, request a "lite" or low-fat dressing. If unavailable, request that the dressing be served on the side so that you can monitor the amount used. (You'll find that if you dip your fork into the dressing first and then into the salad, you'll consume less dressing with each mouthful than if you spoon the dressing directly onto the salad.)
19. For after-dinner treats, select fruit, angel food cake, Jell-O, sherbet, or sorbet, if available. If not, select a fruit pie (NOT a cream pie) and eat only the filling, since most of the fat is in the crust or pastry.
20. Before attending a party or buffet, eat a low-fat snack. This trick will help you avoid overindulging on high-fat snacks due to hunger and lack of will-power.
21. When traveling by airplane, arrange in advance for a low-fat, low-cholesterol meal to be served to you while aboard the plane. Many airlines provide this service.
22. Finally, do not hesitate to make your special requests known! You will be pleasantly surprised that most restaurants will go the extra mile to accommodate you. Remember, it's your life and your health that's at stake—so TAKE CHARGE!

 *Index*